# RAISING EMOTIONALLY HEALTHY CHILDREN

The author's earnings from sales of this book will be given to the St Patrick's Mental Health Foundation in support of the Walk in My Shoes campaign that raises funds for services to help people with mental health difficulties in Ireland.

# RAISING EMOTIONALLY HEALTHY CHILDREN

**PAUL GILLIGAN**

VERITAS

Published 2015 by
Veritas Publications
7–8 Lower Abbey Street
Dublin 1, Ireland
publications@veritas.ie
www.veritas.ie

ISBN 978 1 84730 591 6
Copyright © Paul Gilligan, 2015

10 9 8 7 6 5 4 3 2

A catalogue record for this book is available from the British Library.

Cover Design by Heather Costello, Veritas
Printed in the Republic of Ireland by Watermans Printers Ltd, Cork

Veritas books are printed on paper made from the wood pulp of managed forests. For every tree felled, at least one tree is planted, thereby renewing natural resources.

To Lorraine

# Contents

# Acknowledgements

My thanks and gratitude are due to a number of people:

Firstly to all of those children and parents I have worked with over the years, who have taught me so much and who have impressed upon me the importance of parental love.

To Brendan Power, Aine Lynch, Emma Mc Kinley, Sarah Surgenor, Brian Greene and Rhona Barnett who read so many drafts and gave me invaluable advice. To Audrey Cunningham, Fergus Finlay, Mary Kennedy, Jim Lucey, Tom Maher, Jillian Van Turnout and Tanya Ward for their help.

To the team in Veritas, in particular Donna Doherty, Daragh Reddin and Marie O'Neill, and to Tom Costello and Atlantic Philanthropies for their support.

To Brian, Dolores, Maureen and Tony.

Most importantly to my wife Lorraine and my daughters Katie and Aisling for their love, support and inspiration.

# Introduction

'Loving our child comes naturally. "Naturally" takes work.'

Being emotionally healthy is vital to our overall happiness and to our ability to live an enjoyable and fulfilling life. The evidence tells us that children who are emotionally healthy and psychologically resilient are less likely to experience emotional difficulties and are more likely to overcome these difficulties if they occur.

Working as a clinical psychologist with children and teenagers for over twenty-five years and running a large mental health service has taught me that for children, love is the essence of emotional well-being. Children who love themselves and are loved, particularly by their parents, have a healthier sense of emotional well-being and stronger psychological resilience.

This book explores the concept of 'loving our child' and how we can connect with and utilise this love to help our child to be an emotionally healthy person. It explores how we can teach children to love themselves and how this love helps them to lead emotionally healthy lives. How we can best prevent and manage the emotional difficulties our child might encounter is explored alongside the importance of keeping ourselves emotionally healthy. Each chapter is prefaced by a brief reflection in which I blend my own thoughts on parenthood with those of parents I have spoken to during my course of work.

Parenting is a journey of discovery through which we learn more about our child and ourselves each day. This book aims to help in this discovery journey. Throughout the book there are exercises aimed at encouraging us to think about our special relationship with our child, their emotional well-being, our parenting approach and our own emotional well-being. Each question is designed to help us reflect on an aspect of our child or of our parenting. Each exercise is self-contained and help sheets in processing them are provided throughout the book*. How to piece together the lessons from all these exercises is outlined in the final chapter.

The central message of the book is one of empowerment and optimism. All children have the capacity to live emotionally healthy lives and parents play a key role in influencing and nurturing this. All of us have the capacity to be successful parents once we connect with our self-belief and natural parenting ability.

*Should parents like to complete these exercises online or print off copies they can also be found at www.workbook.ie.

# one

## *Finding Our Inner Parent*

'I know from being a father that becoming a parent changes your life forever. You think about your children every day. There is never a time when you are free from their influence. Your life is never your own again and it is fantastic. You wonder how you ever lived without them.'

**What is our 'inner parent'?**

Our 'inner parent' is that part of us where our natural love for our child meets our natural ability to parent. It is the realisation that we love our child, that we were born to parent our child and that despite the challenges we face, nothing will ever stop us from loving and doing our best for our child.

Finding our inner parent is essential if we are to begin the journey towards building our child's emotional health and psychological resilience. When we connect with our inner parent, we connect with a core component of our self-identity and self-value, realising that being a parent is an innate part of our make up. This realisation can happen at any age and at any stage in the parenting journey.

Our inner parent has three distinct features: loving our child unconditionally; valuing the uniqueness of our child; and believing in our natural parenting ability.

*Loving our child unconditionally:* love for our child is natural; it is always in us. Connecting with this inner love can happen at any stage in the parenting journey. Some parents describe 'falling in love' with their baby while for others it emerges gradually. A child parented through love is happy, expressive and creative. They are naturally curious about life, can laugh when things are funny and cry when they are sad. They are not terrified of the consequences of their behaviour or focused unnecessarily upon reactions of adults. They are in touch with who they truly are. This child becomes a strong and stable adult, able to deal with conflicting demands and pressures and in time able to raise their own children through love.

*Valuing the uniqueness of our child:* A core component of connecting with our inner parent is believing our child is unique. This reinforces for us that our job is to help our child grow to understand their true selves, to discover who they are and to fulfil themselves in their own unique way.

By acknowledging and valuing our child as the very special person he or she is, we make their full intelligence, abilities and potential available to them. Our child is more likely to be secure and happy, and less likely to be aggressive, distracted and filled with insecurities and fears. Valuing the uniqueness of our child requires taking our lead from him or her and not imposing our expectations, ideas or fears on them.

*Believing in our natural parenting ability:* The concept of natural parenting ability has long been discussed and explored by sociologists and psychologists. The bestselling author and social psychologist Penelope Leach writes in her book *Baby and Child*: 'If you let it, your body will start loving the baby for you. Whatever your mind and the deeply entrenched habits of your previous life may be telling you. Your body's commands and your baby's physical reactions are your best guide to handling him' (Leach, 1988). In her book *The Natural Child*, Jan Hunt, the Canadian psychologist, explores the idea of instinctive parenting, the central principle of which is that the utmost sensitivity to our child's innate emotional and physical needs stems from our natural, innate rearing capability (Hunt J. 2001). Central to our inner parent is recognising this natural ability and believing that it will be awakened when we emotionally connect with and commit to our child.

Finding this belief involves self-awareness, self-confidence and a capacity for self-reflection. It involves using the energy of our natural love for our child to connect with that part of us that will always do what we think is right for him or her. We may not always know what is right and may need help or advice with the options; we may sometimes make wrong choices, but we will always know what feels right and try to do this.

| **EXERCISE: CONNECTING WITH OUR INNER PARENT** |
| --- |
| Take no more than three minutes to complete each of these questions as honestly as you can. Move on to the next question after three minutes and leave any you can't complete unanswered. Do the exercise for each of your children separately. |
| **YOUR CHILD'S NAME:** |

| 1 | When did you first realise you loved him/her? |
| --- | --- |
| 2 | How did this make you feel? |
| 3 | What is it about him/her you love the most? |
| 4 | What is the most unique thing about him/her? |
| 5 | What is it about him/her you enjoy the most? |
| 6 | As a parent, what comes naturally to you? |

The purpose of this exercise is to help us reflect on and reconnect with our innate love for our child. It is not an easy exercise to complete because it requires us to consider what we often take for granted or have not fully recognised. It asks us to articulate our deep and personal feelings towards our child, and from this perspective it can be challenging.

The process of completing the questions and reflecting on our answers gives us an opportunity to remember and reinforce the special feeling we have for our child. This serves to reinvigorate our parenting.

Reflecting on unanswered questions is also very constructive. These may indicate that we are only commencing the journey of discovering our inner parent or that we find it difficult to express how we feel about our child. Being able to articulate our feelings for our child is not in itself important, but the process of recognising and connecting with these feelings is. We ourselves will know why we have not been able to find the answers. Whatever the reason, unanswered questions provide us with an opportunity to start to explore or re-explore our love for our child within ourselves.

The exercise should also be considered from the context of how connecting with our feelings for our child is a core component of helping them become emotionally healthy. Knowing they are loved is important to our child's emotional welfare and connecting with this love enables us to provide this.

Difficult as it is, completing this exercise represents the beginning of the parenting journey and is worth careful consideration. It can also be worthwhile to revisit our answers in the future, particularly at times of parenting challenges.

## Connecting with our 'inner parent'

Connecting with our inner parent requires three psychological capacities: self-awareness; cognitive awareness; and growth acceptance.

*Parenting Self-Awareness: Knowing and understanding ourselves*
Parenting self-awareness is the ability to know and understand ourselves as a parent. It involves insight into why we decided to become a parent, our feelings about being a parent, and what we expect from ourselves as a parent.

The decision to become a parent primarily arises from love of a partner, a desire to have and love a child, and a sense that the time is right to start or expand our family. We enter into a contract with our child to love and nurture them and with our partner to cherish another person together. We may not always be explicitly aware that we are making these contracts; sometimes they are made unconsciously, but they are made nonetheless.

Reconnecting with our decision and with the special investment we have made awakens the special feelings we have for our child. When difficulties arise or when we start feeling stressed and disillusioned, this awareness can reinvigorate us and enable us to put negative feelings into perspective. It helps put into context the inevitable changes parenting involves, the emotions parenting evokes, and the many demands of parenting.

Exploring why we decided to become a parent can sometimes initially produce negative answers, and this might suggest that we have not looked deeply enough into ourselves. There are many different levels at which the question can be considered and often the answers change as we grow to understand ourselves better as parents. Giving birth to or adopting a baby is a major life change and, understandably, requires adjustment. The world-renowned paediatrician and pioneer in infant psychotherapy T. Berry Brazelton discusses the birth of attachment commencing at the first stirrings of the desire for a child through the fantasies and work of pregnancy (Brazelton. TB. 1991). A similar process occurs when a child is being adopted. Deep within us there is always a core personal reason for choosing to become a parent. Essential to the process of connecting with our inner parent is the search for the true answers as to why we made this decision to become a parent and resolving any negative feelings we might have around it. Of course sometimes the circumstances of becoming pregnant are not positive. While this needs to be resolved we nonetheless need to acknowledge that we still made the decision to become a parent. Exploring why we chose this option is important.

Our reasons for becoming a parent do not predetermine our attitudes to parenting. These change when our child arrives and are shaped by our interaction and relationship with our child. So another important component of parenting self-awareness is our feelings about being a parent: how good or competent we believe we are as parents, how much satisfaction we are getting out of parenting, and how being a parent fits with the image we have of ourselves.

Connecting with our inner parent involves believing that we are the best people to parent our own child. This is influenced by the reinforcement we receive from our child but also by how competent we believe we are as people and the reinforcement we get from others, particularly our parenting partner, if we have one. Our beliefs will also be determined by the satisfaction we get from parenting. If we are deriving happiness and satisfaction from our parenting, we will believe we are good parents.

Our image of ourselves changes when we become a parent. We become a 'mammy' or 'daddy'. We become aware that other people's image of us changes. Many of us embrace the idea of being a parent, integrating this role into our self-image and adapting to the life changes it entails. We enjoy being seen as a parent by others and start to engage and interact more with others who share our parenting interests.

Some parents actively resist defining themselves as a parent while others define themselves solely as parents, ignoring the other components of themselves and their lives. Having difficulty defining ourselves as a parent can cause detachment from our child and from our inner parent, while defining ourselves completely as a parent can lead to over-attachment. It is important that we are comfortable with seeing ourselves as a parent while being confident that this does not solely define us as a person. Integrating the image of ourselves as a parent into our image of ourselves as a person is important.

Having a balanced and reasonable expectation of ourselves is key to connecting with our inner parent. While we endeavour to do our best for our child, we will do some things right and we will make many mistakes. Having expectations of ourselves as parents is important to ensure we work to do what is best for our child, but if our expectations are too high, we will inevitably fail to live up to them and will become disillusioned.

It is important that our parenting expectations are our own and not our parents', our friends' or our partner's. It is also essential that we confront and challenge any unreasonable parenting expectations placed upon us. Attempting to live up to these expectations creates unnecessary barriers to connecting with our inner parent.

| **EXERCISE: PARENTING SELF-AWARENESS** |
| Take no more than three minutes to complete each of these questions as honestly as you can. Move on to the next question after three minutes and leave any you can't complete unanswered. Do the exercise for each of your children separately. |

| 7 | Why did you decide to have your child? |
|---|---|
| 8 | How do you feel about being a parent to him/her? |
| 9 | What are you good at as a parent to him/her? |
| 10 | What do you enjoy about being a parent to him/her? |
| 11 | What do you feel you could be better at as a parent to him/her? |
| 12 | What else are you good at other than being a parent? |

This exercise seeks to help us explore our motivations for deciding to become parents and how we feel about being parents. It can be challenging because it requires us to explore very personal decisions. Reflecting on our answers to these questions reminds us that no matter what the circumstances of our pregnancy or adoption, becoming a parent was an active decision. The answers also help us to recognise our strengths and acknowledge things we would like to improve on as parents. The last question in this exercise is designed to help us identify other strengths we might have and should not lose sight off.

Considering the questions we couldn't answer is also beneficial. Our inability to answer may simply be arising from a difficulty in articulating our motivations for becoming parents and our strengths and abilities as parents. However, our difficulty answering some of these questions may also reflect where we are in the parenting self-awareness journey. Unanswered questions give us an opportunity to commence exploration of one of the most important aspects of parenting: why we made the decision to become a parent. Difficulties in answering questions nine to twelve may suggest that we have become too focused on the negative aspects of parenting or have become too focused on parenting itself and have lost sight of other aspects of ourselves. Again this insight is an opportunity for us to redress this imbalance in our parenting outlook.

For this exercise in particular it is vital to remember that parenting is a journey of discovery and that our answers need to be considered in the context of this.

Our parenting self-awareness will inevitably impact on our ability to support our child's emotional well-being and this makes exploring these aspects of ourselves very important no matter how challenging.

## Cognitive awareness: exploring and resolving our belief systems about our child

To connect with our inner parent we must believe that our child has an unlimited potential to achieve and has tremendous ability to live a happy and healthy life.

Our beliefs about our child will be influenced by our personal belief systems about children. These, while continually changing and evolving, are primarily influenced by three factors: our experience of being a child ourselves; our experience of being parents; societal beliefs about children.

### Our own childhood

Our own childhood is probably the single most influential factor in determining how we view and interact with our child. Developing an awareness of the positive and negative impact our childhood has had on us, and whether we have resolved the emotional legacy of these experiences, is crucial. If, as a child, we saw ourselves as clever and good, it will be easier for us to see our child as being this way. If, on the other hand, as a child we saw ourselves in a negative way, it can be very difficult for us to see our own child positively.

Positive experiences in our own childhood make it easier to have positive beliefs about children, and while negative experiences in childhood do not prevent us from having a positive belief system about our child, it is important to ensure that the emotional impact of any negative experiences has been resolved as best it can. This requires insight, honesty and commitment.

Exploring our personal childhood experiences is not about deciding if our childhood was healthy or not. It is, rather, a process of accepting that what constitutes our childhood is a combination of positive and negative experiences that shape our ideas of what it is to be a child. We need to learn from these positive and negative experiences. We also need to explore the impact of how we ourselves were parented – our 'parenting legacy' – on our belief systems about parenting.

## Our experience of being parents

Parenting is a circular process. How we parent our child influences our attitudes and beliefs about our child, which in turn impacts on our parenting. From the moment of birth, a child influences our self-worth, emotional well-being and psychological resilience.

How we parent one child impacts significantly on how we perceive and interact with our other children. Each child will have their own unique personality but we will nonetheless apply the experiences we have gained from each to the others. If our confidence has been reinforced by our experiences with our first child, this will make us more confident parenting our second. Setbacks experienced with the first child will need to be understood and overcome with the second.

## Societal beliefs about children

We do not parent in a vacuum. All around us there are different ideas and attitudes about children. Institutions such as schools, churches and the judicial system all have particular cultures that shape society's view of children. It is important to be aware that there are many different types of beliefs about children within all of the organisations and institutions which impact on our child's life and our own lives. Being able to identify what these beliefs are, to embrace or challenge them, to ensure they impact positively on our child, is important. For instance, every school has a set of belief systems about children that are enshrined in its rulebook and underscored by its accepted practices. Some schools may deem children who don't conform as incapable of changing their ways and so encourage them to leave education prematurely. Other schools try to nurture and embrace these children and attempt to find ways to help them integrate. Societal beliefs about children are constantly evolving and parents can influence them to ensure these beliefs are challenged and remain healthy.

| **EXERCISE:** EXPLORING OUR BELIEF SYSTEMS | |
|---|---|
| Take no more than three minutes to complete each of these questions as honestly as you can. Move on to the next question after three minutes and leave any you can't complete unanswered. | |
| 13 | What was the most positive thing about your own childhood? |
| 14 | What was the most negative thing about your own childhood? |
| 15 | What have you learnt from your own parents that you use in your parenting? |
| 16 | What have you decided not to do in your own parenting that your parents did? |
| 17 | What have you learnt from your child about parenting? |
| 18 | What have you learnt from your friends about parenting? |
| 19 | What is good about where you live for parenting? |

This exercise is designed to help us explore some of the key influences on our belief systems about children and childhood. The most challenging aspect of this exercise is our ability to be as honest as we can with ourselves regarding some of the more sensitive questions.

The first four questions of this exercise explore how our own experiences of childhood might be impacting on our parenting belief systems and approach. The last two questions explore current influences on our parenting. Our answers to the first four questions help us to acknowledge that we all inevitably bring both positive and negative influences from our own childhood to our current parenting outlook. The answers to the last two questions help us to consider our ability to learn about our parenting on a day-to-day basis, both from our child and from our friends.

Reflecting on questions we could not answer is equally as important. If we feel that our inability to answer the first four questions is related to our reluctance or inability to explore this aspect of our lives then we need to acknowledge this and confront the subject. Over the course of our parenting journey we will at some stage benefit from resolving our own childhood experiences. Our inability to answer the last two questions in this exercise is also worth considering in the context of assessing whether we find it easy to learn about our parenting from our experiences.

Supporting our child to become emotionally healthy will at some stage require us to assess the impact of our own childhood experiences and to have the ability to reflect on and learn from our day-to-day parenting.

## Growth acceptance: parenting is ever evolving

The third key component of connecting with our inner parent is the ability to develop and grow as a person. Parenting is an ever-changing and evolving relationship requiring a willingness to work hard, learn and improve. As our child grows and develops, the opportunities and challenges of parenting change. Each child we parent is different and is parented in differing circumstances. To respond we must be willing to grow. This growth brings great satisfaction and joy to our lives and enhances us as people.

The growth journey involves having the self-awareness to know that we need to continually develop. It involves having the courage to take on change. It requires being honest with ourselves about what we know and do not know and being prepared to acquire the necessary knowledge and skills.

| **EXERCISE:** PARENTING GROWTH | |
|---|---|
| Take no more than three minutes to complete each of these questions as honestly as you can. Move on to the next question after three minutes and leave any you can't complete unanswered. Do the exercise for each of your children separately. | |
| 20 | What would you like to improve about the way you parent? |
| 21 | What aspect of parenting would you like to know more about? |
| 22 | What aspect of parenting in the future are you looking forward to? |
| 23 | What aspect of parenting in the future are you concerned about? |
| 24 | What would you like to do to improve your parenting? |
| 25 | What extra support would you like to help you parent? |

This exercise is designed to help us reflect on our ability and willingness to learn and develop as parents. The answers we give to this exercise can help us to map out our own parenting development plan. It also helps us to acknowledge that none of us are perfect parents and that we all have the capacity to learn and improve.

Unanswered questions can also give us some useful insights. Perhaps we do not see too many areas of parenting which we can improve on at the moment, or perhaps we are finding parenting particularly challenging and stressful. If we believe we are experiencing the latter it might be appropriate for us to talk to somebody we trust about our concerns and to seek support. Developing this insight is in itself very useful. Unanswered questions in this exercise are particularly useful to revisit when our parenting circumstances change.

Being able to support our child's healthy emotional development will require us to be flexible and adaptable in our parenting approach. Being able to acknowledge our parenting growth needs will greatly enhance these abilities.

**Summary**

Finding our inner parent is the essential first part of the journey towards creating emotionally healthy children. It is a journey worth making, connecting us with our unconditional love for our child, the special uniqueness of our child, and giving us a renewed confidence in our natural ability to parent.

Finding our inner parent is not a state of being. It is a lifelong journey of self-growth and enhancement requiring courage and commitment. It involves making a commitment to assessing and evaluating our deepest beliefs about ourselves as parents throughout our lives.

# two

## *Teaching Our Children How to be Happy:*
### *Building Emotional Awareness and Psychological Resilience*

'It's watching my children dancing that I find so fulfilling. They get lost in the music and their self-expression. I know that they have found that very special place within themselves. The place of knowing how to be happy and how to enjoy life.'

So the first step towards creating emotionally healthy children is connecting with our inner parent. The next essential part of the journey is putting this love into practice. This involves doing two things: teaching our child how to be happy and content and to have a positive outlook on life; and teaching our child how to have positive self-belief.

Psychological research the world over indicates that children who are happy and who feel good about themselves will be emotionally healthy and psychologically resilient. No matter what their personalities, social networks or life experiences, these children will be best equipped to deal with their emotional lives. The psychologist Robert Burns, drawing from the work of renowned researchers such as Seligman 1975, Bandura 1977 and Bowlby 1980, identifies how the beliefs and evaluations people hold about themselves determine who they are, what they can do and what they can become. He discusses how these powerful inner influences provide an internal guiding mechanism steering and nurturing individuals through life and governing their behaviour (Burns 1982).

While the ability to be happy and feel good about ourselves are each important in their own right, it is the combination of the two that creates sustainable and robust emotional health. As

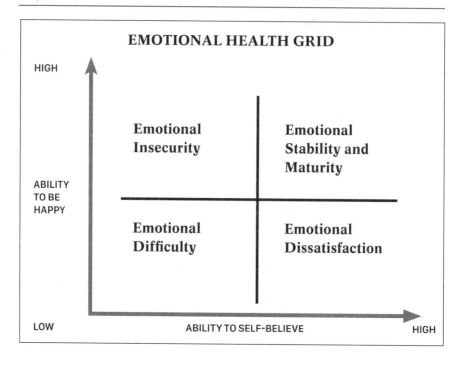

EMOTIONAL HEALTH GRID

HIGH

ABILITY TO BE HAPPY

Emotional Insecurity

Emotional Stability and Maturity

Emotional Difficulty

Emotional Dissatisfaction

LOW

ABILITY TO SELF-BELIEVE

HIGH

the Emotional Health Grid indicates, children who have learned how to be happy and to feel good about themselves will have high emotional intelligence and will be emotionally stable and mature. Children who have low self-belief are more likely to be insecure, overly compliant and emotionally brittle, being extremely sensitive to the views and whims of others. Children whose ability to be happy is very low are more likely to get stressed or downhearted, never being satisfied with how they feel. Children who have low self-belief combined with low ability to be happy will tend to have low emotional intelligence, low self-esteem and will be at greater risk of developing emotional difficulties.

**Teaching our child how to be happy**
When a person is happy they are more likely to be healthy, expressive, creative and in touch with who they truly are. Happy children are naturally curious about life, experiencing each day as an adventure. These are children to whom sharing comes naturally; who can laugh when things are funny and cry when they're sad; who are not terrified of the consequences of their behaviour or focused unnecessarily upon reactions of adults. These children have the best

chance of becoming emotionally strong and stable, able to weather all kinds of conflicting demands, pressures and challenges.

Teaching our child how to be happy does not mean that they will be happy all the time. It is teaching them how to enjoy their lives at an appropriate level and at appropriate times and to see the good that is in their lives. Happiness is not a state of being; rather it is a state of mind. All of us need to learn how to be happy, how to enjoy and how to appreciate life.

## Promoting individualism

Recognising and treating our child as an individual in their own right is an important part of the parenting process. Children are born with their own personalities and, no matter what age, will have their own opinions, beliefs and feelings. Promoting our child's individualism involves nurturing their self-expression, reinforcing their personal characteristics and giving them the freedom to 'be themselves'. Avoiding comparisons and conformity with other children is central to this process.

Involving children as much as we can as active participants in the parenting process also nurtures individualism and empowers them. This means including them fully in decision-making at an age-appropriate level, allowing them to freely express their views and opinions, and ensuring these are taken into account.

Accepting and treating our child as a young person with their own unique personality not only helps him/her to see happiness in themselves but also enhances the vitality and richness of our relationship with them.

## Seeing the best in our child

Looking for and seeing the best in our child and all that they do is an important part of teaching them how to be happy. A child who believes they are in essence a good person will find it easier to be happy and to recognise happiness. Even when they make mistakes, helping them to realise that they are good and special is essential. A child who can see the best in themselves will not only find it easier to appreciate happiness, but will also be better able to cope with criticism and negativity.

| | **EXERCISE: CHILD PERSONALITY CHECKLIST** |
|---|---|
| | Take no more than three minutes to complete each of these questions as honestly as you can. Move on to the next question after three minutes and leave any you can't complete unanswered. Do the exercise for each of your children separately. |

| 26 | What characteristics make your child special? |
|---|---|
| 27 | How does he/she express these? |
| 28 | What does your child like to do to relax? |
| 29 | What makes your child laugh? |
| 30 | What does your child do particularly well? |
| 31 | What decisions do you let your child make for him/herself? |

The aim of this exercise is to help us reflect on how much consideration we give to our child's individual personality. It can be an enjoyable process identifying what makes our child special. The answers not only remind us that we know our child best but also gives us the opportunity to remember that our child has his/her own unique characteristics and ways of expressing them.

If we find it difficult to answer some of these questions or have left some unanswered this may suggest that we have not given this aspect of our parenting a great deal of thought before now or that perhaps we have lost some focus on our child. The unanswered questions therefore provide us with the opportunity to further consider or reconnect with our child's very special personality. If we find our answers to these questions drifting into negative aspects of our child this could perhaps indicate that we are finding parenting challenging at present. If this is the case we need to try to focus more attention on the positive aspects of our child's personality or to resolve the issues that are causing the negativity.

Recognising and acknowledging our child's positive personality traits is a vital component of building their emotional health.

**Helping our child know and understand themselves**

Learning how to be happy requires that we understand ourselves and have an accurate and positive sense of ourselves – we call this self-awareness. Although building self-awareness is a lifelong process, it starts the moment a child is born. Developing a sense of self and an ability to self-reflect will vary at different ages but is particularly important for children. The earlier a child starts to develop self-awareness skills, the more at ease they will become with themselves as they grow. The stronger the foundations of self-awareness, the harder it is to shake or unhinge them. Helping our child build self-awareness involves using everyday parenting skills but with a different focus. As with all aspects of parenting, these skills and our role will change as our child develops. A child's self-awareness is influenced by many factors but parents play the key role in helping their child develop this important life skill.

**Developing the ability to recognise, understand and deal with their own and other people's emotions**

Linked to self-awareness is emotional intelligence or the ability to recognise, understand and deal with our own and other people's emotions. Helping our child develop strong emotional intelligence is important in assisting them to learn how to be happy. If our child has strong emotional intelligence, they will be better equipped to recognise happiness, sadness and stress. Recognising these emotions makes them easier to manage. Strong emotional intelligence also helps our child understand and respond better to other people's emotions. The earlier a child starts to develop this ability, the more likely they are to be emotionally healthy and to cope with psychological challenges. Developing strong emotional intelligence is a lifelong process and again a parent's role in helping their children develop this ability continues throughout their lives.

The following table outlines ways in which children can be helped to develop their self-awareness and emotional intelligence at different stages of their life.

| HELP SHEET: Developing Self-awareness and Emotional-intelligence | | | | |
|---|---|---|---|---|
| **Talking about themselves and their interactions with others**<br><br>Encouraging a child to talk about themselves and their interactions with others helps them develop a sense of who they are and what they are like. It also helps them understand the type of person they are in relation to others. | **Expressing and understanding feelings**<br><br>Children encouraged to express their feelings in a positive way will have a better sense of themselves and of how they understand and experience emotion. Helping them explore where these feelings come from and how to resolve them is also important. Understanding the feelings of others is part of this process. | **Celebrating their strengths**<br><br>Children who learn and have insight into what they are genuinely good at will develop a better, more positive sense of themselves and of their feelings. By recognising what they are good at, they will become aware of and be accepting of their weaknesses. | **Nurturing self-reflection skills**<br><br>Helping children to reflect on their actions, statements and feelings gives them a better understanding of themselves and their emotions. | **Nurturing and discussing values**<br><br>Developing a sense of what we believe is right or wrong is an important part of developing self-awareness and emotional intelligence. |
| **0–4 YEARS**<br>Talking about their day from their perspective, no matter how basic the information. | Allowing them to cry, have tantrums, laugh, be excited and interpreting these behaviours for them: 'You're crying because you're tired/you're jumping because you're happy'. | Recognising what they are good at and telling them. 'You are kind for giving Sean a hug when he hurt himself.' 'You are good at art, look at the lovely picture you drew.' | Guiding concrete reflection. 'I think you did that because you are angry.' | Guiding concrete values. 'I think it is wrong to take somebody else's sweets. Or 'I think it is good to hug your sister when she is sad'. |
| **4–12 YEARS**<br>Talking about themselves and their friends and siblings and how this makes them feel about themselves. | Encouraging them to express their emotions through words and helping them interpret their feelings through guidance. | Encouraging them to engage in what they think they are good at. | Asking them concrete reflection questions and guiding them to answer, e.g. 'Why were you unhappy after school? Was it because you were tired?' | Giving them concrete value guidance and seeking their views. 'I don't think it's right that John hurt that other boy. What do you think?' |
| **12–16 YEARS**<br>Talking about the key things that happen to them in their day from their perspective but focusing on how they interpret these events in the context of their self-image. | Allowing them to express their emotions and encouraging them to interpret these themselves. | Helping them commit to what they are good at and giving them support and encouragement in this area. | Asking specific reflection questions: 'How are you feeling about the row you had last night? Why do you think it happened?' | Asking specific value questions. 'Do you think what happened in school yesterday was right? Why/why not?' |
| **16–21 YEARS**<br>Enabling them to discuss how they see and feel about themselves and how others make them feel. Supporting them when their views are accurate and challenging them gently when they are inaccurate. | Enabling them to discuss their feelings and what causes these feelings. Supporting and challenging them when appropriate. | Supporting them to pursue their strengths and helping them overcome setbacks. | Supporting self-reflection without influence or interference: 'How are you feeling? Why do you think that is?' | Supporting self-exploration of values without influence or judgement: 'So you feel that is right/ so you feel that is wrong.' |

**EXERCISE: SELF-AWARENESS AND EMOTIONAL INTELLIGENCE**

Take no more than three minutes to complete each of these questions as honestly as you can. Move on to the next question after three minutes and leave any you can't complete unanswered. Do the exercise for each of your children separately.

| 32 | What about him/herself does your child like to talk about? |
|---|---|
| 33 | What about him/herself do they not like to talk about? |
| 34 | What does he/she say and do when happy? |
| 35 | What does he/she say and do when sad? |
| 36 | What does he/she think they are good at? |
| 37 | What does he/she think they are weak at? |
| 38 | What makes him/her angry with himself/herself? |
| 39 | What stops him/her being angry with himself/herself? |
| 40 | What one thing does he/she think is right? |
| 41 | What one thing does he/she think is wrong? |

The purpose of this exercise is to help us explore how aware we are of our child's self-image and of his/her emotional development. Our answers to these questions helps us to focus on the importance of being aware of how our child expresses various emotions, particularly positive ones, and how both their self-image and self-awareness are developing. If we found answering the questions about negative emotions or self-image easier than the positive, we need to consider whether this suggests our child is more focused on negative emotions and negative self-image or whether we are focused on these aspects of our child's personality. This may initiate a refocusing of our attention or may require additional work with our children to help them focus on the positive aspects of their personalities.

Unanswered questions serve as a reminder for us to reconsider the attention we are paying to this aspect of our child's development. To support our child's emotional well-being and development, we need to be sensitive to how they express emotion. They themselves also need to be aware of how they express emotion and how they view themselves.

The answers to this particular exercise will change throughout the parenting journey and, from this perspective, this exercise is worth revisiting.

## Shaping our child's thinking and behaviour

One of the most important determinants of how children learn to be happy is how they think about things and how their behaviour influences and is influenced by this thinking. Children from a very early age begin to develop an emotional mindset which they use to understand and deal with their life experiences. This mindset is influenced by the personality with which they are born, as well as by those skills they learn or are taught to emotionally interpret events and actions. Helping our child to develop an accurate, positive emotional mindset is important in teaching them how to be happy. While every child will have distinctly positive and negative experiences in their lives, most everyday experiences are open to interpretation. Teaching our child how to be happy involves us shaping their thinking to enable them to recognise, support and embrace a positive mindset.

Supporting and helping our child to interpret their actions is also important to this process. We know that our actions and how we interpret them influences how we think about things, so encouraging children to engage in activities or behaviours that they find relaxing and enjoyable is essential. Likewise, helping them interpret their activities and actions in a positive way is also important.

| HELP SHEET: Shaping Thinking and Behaviour | | | |
|---|---|---|---|
| **Modelling positive thinking and actions** | **Rewarding positive thinking and actions** | **Teaching reframing skills** | **Teaching problem-solving skills** |
| How we think, act and interpret our actions is a key influence on how our child thinks and acts. | Showing we value positive thinking and actions will encourage our child to engage in these types of thinking and actions. | Seeing the positives in events and crises is a skill best taught by parents. | Helping our child find solutions to problems that arise helps keep a focus on the positive. |
| **0–4 YEARS** Engaging in concrete positive actions such as smiling and laughing, and making concrete positive statements, i.e. 'I am happy today because it's sunny and we are going to the playground.' | Paying attention to positive actions and reinforcing this through responding with our own positive actions. Ignoring negative actions. | Reframing events in a concrete way for our child. 'It's sad your lollipop fell on the ground but it was good you had eaten most of it anyway.' | Engaging with our child in concrete problem-solving. 'Well, your juice spilt so let's clean it up, get you some more and put a proper lid on the cup to stop it happening again.' |
| **4–12 YEARS** Showing and telling our child when we are enjoying ourselves. | Paying attention to positive statements and responding with positive statements of our own. Ignoring negative statements. | Helping our child to reframe events for themselves, 'I know you are upset that you lost the match and that's understandable but did you enjoy the game? Do you think you played well?' | Helping our child to problem-solve and find solutions for themselves. 'So you can't find your yellow hair bobbin, what do you think we should do?' |
| **12–16 YEARS** Discussing with our child what makes us happy and gives us enjoyment. | Discussing what actions and thoughts make him/her feel good and positive about life. | Supporting positive reframing when he/she engages in it, 'I am disappointed I wasn't invited to that party but I am not very friendly with that girl anyway and I am always invited to my friends' parties'. | Supporting positive problem-solving when he/she engages in it, 'I missed the last class today because of my dental appointment but I rang my friend to get the homework questions.' |
| **16–21 YEARS** Discussing the concepts of enjoyment, contentment and happiness with our child. | Discussing the concepts of thinking and acting positively and what they mean for our child. | Discussing the principles behind positive reframing, – how you can change your views of things to view them positively and reinforcing this practice. | Discussing and reinforcing the concepts of positive problem-solving, such as focusing on finding solutions or accepting that situations cannot be changed and agreeing on alternative options. |

**EXERCISE: SHAPING THINKING AND BEHAVIOUR**

Take no more than three minutes to complete each of these questions as honestly as you can. Move on to the next question after three minutes and leave any you can't complete unanswered. Do the exercise for each of your children separately.

| 42 | What's the main thing you do that shows your child you are happy? |
|----|---|
| 43 | What's the main thing you say that shows him/her you are happy? |
| 44 | What do you encourage your child to do that makes him/her happy? |
| 45 | What do you encourage your child to say that makes him/her happy? |
| 46 | How do you encourage your child to see things positively? |
| 47 | How do you encourage your child to do things positively? |
| 48 | How do you encourage your child to find solutions to problems? |

This exercise focuses on the skills of modelling and reinforcement. Our answers to the first two questions help us to consider how we model being content and happy to our child. Our answers can help us to see how effective we are at this aspect of our parenting and can encourage us to continue with this practice and to identify any opportunities for further development. Our answers to the remaining five questions help us to focus on what we do to reinforce positive behaviour and thinking in our child. Again, our answers to these questions can provide us with reassurance that we are shaping positive behaviour and can enable us to recognise developmental opportunities.

Reflecting on the questions we found difficult or could not answer is also constructive and may suggest that we need to give this aspect of our parenting more thought or indeed that this aspect of our parenting requires a little more development. Unanswered questions give us the opportunity to begin the very important process of finding out how to focus or develop our skills in this area.

The skills of shaping thinking and behaviour are an essential component of parenting children to be emotionally healthy.

## Summary

Teaching our child how to be happy is essential to their long-term emotional health and psychological resilience. This is not a difficult task, and it is enjoyable and fulfilling because it makes us happier parents. Having the ability to be happy does not mean that our child will be happy all of the time or will ignore sad or hurtful emotions. It will, however, arm our child to see the good in life and to enjoy life when the opportunity arises. It will prepare our child better for the challenges of life and will enable them to recognise and cope better with negative emotions.

# three

## Teaching Our Children Self-Belief

'Nothing is as heartening as witnessing the young lad who's not the best footballer volunteering to take the penalty. His belief in himself exceeds all fear or social expectations. You know he is having a good childhood and that he is moving towards a fulfilling adult life.'

As discussed in chapter one, our job as parents is to help our children grow to understand their true selves, to discover who they are and to seek fulfilment in their own unique way. Parenting children is a process of discovery in which we give our child the space to grow to be themselves while giving ourselves the opportunity to discover and learn about them.

All children have their own inherent wisdom, abilities, curiosity and sense of what is important to them. When a child's basic nature is allowed to flourish they will be emotionally healthy and psychologically resilient, and parents have a unique role to play in this process.

### Expressing our love for them

Telling and showing our child we love them as often as possible makes a big difference, no matter what age they are. Even on difficult days or after a disagreement, when we might not feel particularly loving, it is most important to reconnect with our love for them and to express it. A child, no matter what age, will feel good about themselves if they believe that they are loved – particularly by their parents – and the easiest way of reinforcing this is by telling and showing them. This is an important means of connecting, which is most effective when done in an age-appropriate, personal manner.

For most children, telling them directly is most effective, but as children get older, how and when we do this can change. Some children like to be shown love through physical contact, while for others a mere smile can be sufficient.

---

**EXERCISE: EXPRESSING OUR LOVE**

Take no more than three minutes to complete each of these questions as honestly as you can. Move on to the next question after three minutes and leave any you can't complete unanswered. Do the exercise for each of your children separately.

---

| 49 | How do you show your child you love them? |
|---|---|
| 50 | What do you say to them to let them know you love them? |
| 51 | How does he/she show you that they love you? |
| 52 | What does he/she say to you to let you know that they love you? |
| 53 | When is the last time you showed your child you loved them? |
| 54 | When is the last time you told your child you loved them? |
| 55 | When you show or tell your child you love him/her, how do they react? |
| 56 | When they show or tell you they love you, how do you react? |
| 57 | When you were a child, how did your parents show and tell you that they loved you? |

This exercise is designed to help us reflect on how we show our child we love him or her. The exercise also helps us to consider how our child expresses their love for us. Our answers to the questions provide us with an opportunity to focus again on the special relationship we have with our child and on how fulfilling this can be. The answers remind us that the best way of making a person feel loved is by telling them or showing them that we love them. Questions fifty-five and fifty-six ask us to reflect on how we respond when our child shows us positive affection and how they respond to our positive affection. This aspect of parenting is important because it indicates that our positive emotions and messages are being understood and appreciated. Similarly, it reminds us of how important it is to give reinforcement to our child that their positive emotions are being understood and appreciated.

The last question in this exercise serves as a reminder to us of how our parents expressed emotion to us and how this will inevitably influence how we show emotion, particularly our love to our child.

The questions we found difficult to answer or could not answer provide us with an opportunity for development. Assessing why we found answering the questions difficult can give us some insight into how we might enhance this area of our parenting. Our difficulty in answering may reflect that we have not looked closely enough at our interactions with our child. It might also suggest that we are finding our parenting challenging at present and as a result do not find it easy to express love. If we feel this is the case it might be appropriate to seek support or to discuss these feelings with somebody we trust.

Building our child's emotional health requires us to be able to express our love to them and to acknowledge when they are expressing their love to us. Reflecting on this exercise from such a perspective is therefore important.

**Spending as much time with our child as they need and want**
Making our child feel that they are a priority in our life greatly enhances their emotional health. The best way to demonstrate this is to spend time together. Our child should, where possible, influence how and when this occurs. We should try our best to be with our child when they need or want us to be. This will change as their lives change, placing great demands on us when they are younger and, less as they grow older. The best time spent together is that which is integral to daily living, with the primary focus on interaction and, where possible, enjoyment. On the following page is a useful guide, but each child and parent will know best what they enjoy doing together.

**HELP SHEET: Spending Time Together**

| | Playing together | Eating together | Making bedtime special | Working together | Having special times together |
|---|---|---|---|---|---|
| | Playing builds our child's sense of self-worth. Younger children usually have fun playing most games, as long as it involves us! It doesn't matter what we play, once we enjoy each other. It is great if we can let our child see our silly, fun side. With older children, we can play more structured games like cards, chess and computer games. We are never too old to play and neither is our child. | Eating together sets the stage for conversation and sharing. When schedules permit, we should really try to eat, talk and enjoy each other's company, even if it is in front of the television. Meals can become a quality time throughout life. | For younger children, reading a favourite bedtime book or telling stories often makes bedtime special. However, older children also need something special. Even with teenagers we need to remember that they still enjoy the ritual of being told 'good night' in a special way by a parent. | Washing the car, choosing which shoes look better with our dress, doing the dishes, or tidying the house are all things that can be done together. Including our child in such activities lets him/her know that we like spending time with them and value their opinion. | It is important to spend special time with each of our children individually: going for a walk, a special trip to a playground, a night at the cinema, shopping together. Although it is more of a challenge the more children there are in a family, it is achievable if we think creatively. |
| **0–4 YEARS** | Face-to-face: smiling, hugging calming, cuddling, tickling, talking and responding. | Eating as many meals as possible together every day. | Reading or telling a story at bedtime. | Doing sensory tasks: baking, washing up together. | Going to the beach, park or for a walk together. |
| **4–12 YEARS** | Playing make-up, dress-up games, one-to-one sports like kicking ball, simple board games together. | Eating breakfast and evening meals together. | Reading and telling a story and talking about the day's events before going to bed. | Cleaning the house, washing the car, doing the dishes together. | Going for a treat, to the playground or to a friend's house together. |
| **12–16 YEARS** | Playing board games, cards, interactive computer games. | Having breakfast or evening meals together. | Talking about the day's events before going to bed, preparing for the next day. | Cleaning the house, washing the car, doing the dishes, doing the gardening together. | Going for a treat, to the cinema, a show, a sports event, or shopping together. |
| **16–21 YEARS** | Having shared hobbies, or playing competitive board games together. | Eating two meals a week, or going out for meals, together. | Talking about the day's events before going to bed, preparing for the next day. | Fixing things, sorting things, printing things on the computer together. | Going for a treat, to the cinema, a show, a sports event, or shopping together. |

Sometimes it is useful to take a look at our lifestyle and the main activities we engage in to get a sense of how balanced it is. One useful way to do this is by using the daily activity chart below.

**Instructions**
Fill in the daily activity chart below based on your average week and for each of your children separately. Mark each hour according to the main activity you are involved in during that hour.

\# For time spent on a hobby
|| For time spent at work
• For time spent with your partner
× For time spent with your child
≠ For time spent with your other children

|  | Mon | Tue | Wed | Thu | Fri | Sat | Sun |
|---|---|---|---|---|---|---|---|
| 08.00 – 09.00 |  |  |  |  |  |  |  |
| 09.00 – 10.00 |  |  |  |  |  |  |  |
| 10.00 – 11.00 |  |  |  |  |  |  |  |
| 11.00 – 12.00 |  |  |  |  |  |  |  |
| 12.00 – 13.00 |  |  |  |  |  |  |  |
| 13.00 – 14.00 |  |  |  |  |  |  |  |
| 14.00 – 15.00 |  |  |  |  |  |  |  |
| 15.00 – 16.00 |  |  |  |  |  |  |  |
| 16.00 – 17.00 |  |  |  |  |  |  |  |
| 17.00 – 18.00 |  |  |  |  |  |  |  |
| 18.00 – 19.00 |  |  |  |  |  |  |  |
| 19.00 – 20.00 |  |  |  |  |  |  |  |
| 20.00 – 21.00 |  |  |  |  |  |  |  |
| 21.00 – 22.00 |  |  |  |  |  |  |  |
| 22.00 – 23.00 |  |  |  |  |  |  |  |
| 23.00 – 24.00 |  |  |  |  |  |  |  |

When you have completed the chart, add up the symbols and fill in the graph below. Reflect on the final graph and consider whether you feel it represents a balanced approach to your parenting.

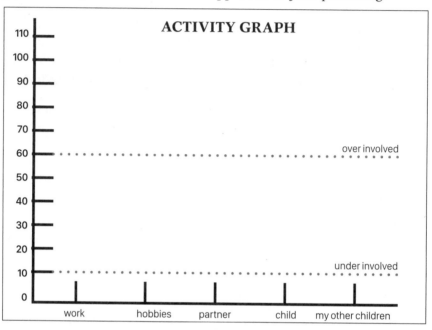

ACTIVITY GRAPH

over involved

under involved

work    hobbies    partner    child    my other children

## Listening and Communication

One of the best and most effective ways of teaching children to feel good about themselves is to listen and communicate with them genuinely, honestly and constructively. Genuine communication involves paying attention to what they are saying, encouraging them to share their thoughts and feelings with us and trying our best to understand fully what they are trying to express. It means paying attention to their actions and behaviours, understanding that this is often how they express their feelings. It involves doing everything we can to understand and to be understood. The practical principles of genuine communication are:

- Listening with concentration and acceptance;
- Asking questions and reflecting back what we understand we are hearing;
- Expressing ourselves in a way that our child can understand.

Honest listening and communication involves being truthful in a constructive manner. It involves expressing love, acknowledging successes, achievements and happiness when we feel these things. It also involves being prepared to deal with the difficult issues and to confront problems. The practical principles of honest communication are:

- Taking responsibility for our own feelings and wishes, by using the 'I' word. 'I feel disappointed because you hit your brother and hurt him – that is why I am not speaking to you;'
- Telling the truth;
- Helping our child take responsibility for their own feelings and wishes, often by getting them to use the 'I' word. 'Tell me how you feel about hitting your brother'.

Perhaps the most important part of good listening and communication is ensuring that it is done constructively. Children, in particular, respond much better to praise, positive reinforcement and support than they do to criticism. Ensuring our communication with them is constructive demonstrates this to them and enhances the likelihood of them engaging with us and others in this way. This is not to say that difficulties, problems or things we want to change cannot be discussed, but it is how this is done that is important. The practical principles of constructive communication are:

- Being empathic – thinking about and considering how what we are going to say will affect our child's feelings, and expressing ourselves with tenderness and compassion;
- Only saying what really needs to be said.

We need to try to avoid the obstacles to honest communication that will arise from time to time. These include disrespecting each other; failing to listen; being too dogmatic; saying one thing but showing another through our actions; jumping to conclusions; and making assumptions. One of the biggest obstacles to communication is secrecy, which is essentially a person refusing to communicate in a constructive way. Of course there are many things it is not appropriate for us to tell our child; however, secrecy involves keeping information he/she should know from them or vice versa. Honest communication does not come easy. It involves continually working to strengthen and enhance our relationships and to remove any blocks that emerge.

Listening to our child takes work because children express themselves differently to adults. It is easy to dismiss what they are saying as silly and assume they do not fully understand. Sometimes they express themselves in ways that we find hurtful because they lack the communication skills that come with age. Seeing through our child's negative, critical statements to try to understand what is actually being expressed is also important to communication.

How we listen will change as our child grows older. If we encourage our child to talk to us when they are young, they will learn that we want to listen. They will know that we care about them and will be much more likely to talk to us as they get older. The chart on the following page outlines some of the skills that are useful at different ages.

## HELP SHEET: Communicating With Our Child

| | Listening | Talking Together | Expressing ourselves through our actions | Helping our child understand their actions as communication |
|---|---|---|---|---|
| | Real listening involves paying attention to what our child is saying and doing to understand fully what they are trying to express, and encouraging them to share their thoughts and feelings with us. | Talking with our child is one of the most important ways to communicate. Saying how we feel and allowing our child to express themselves is essential. | Actions can sometimes speak louder than words. Showing our child how we feel and allowing them to express themselves through age-appropriate actions helps communication. | Seeing our child's actions as communication and indicating to our child that we understand this is important. |
| 0–4 YEARS | Hearing, understanding and responding to crying, and our child's first attempts at speech. | Engaging in word and speaking games and verbal role-play. Reading to our child. | Rocking our baby in a pram or cradle. Walking up and down with him/her. Singing or talking gently to him/her. Cuddling our baby. | Telling our child what we think they are trying to tell us when they have a tantrum or hit out. |
| 4–12 YEARS | Allowing our child to ask all the questions they want and trying to answer them as best we can. | Engaging our child in conversation that interests them by asking lots of questions in a way they can answer. 'What did you do today that you enjoyed?' Telling them about our day. Reading with our child. | Smiling, laughing when we are happy and crying, frowning when we are sad or upset. | Interpreting our child's behaviour and checking with them to see if we have got it right, 'I see you threw your school bag on the ground. I think it's because you're angry – am I right?' |
| 12–16 YEARS | Showing we are actively listening by asking open-ended questions and reflecting back what we think we have heard without making value judgements or giving direction, unless asked. | Discussing our day and asking them about their day, picking up cues to discuss the things they want to discuss. | Interpreting our behaviour for our child, 'I am shouting because I was really worried when you came home so late and did not ring me.' | Asking them to interpret their actions for us, 'When you went upstairs and banged the door just now, what were you feeling?' |
| 16–21 YEARS | Actively listening with empathy and interest and responding supportively. | Discussing things that interest us and encouraging them to do the same. | Discussing with our child how we behave when we are feeling particular things, 'When I am stressed in work I become quiet and withdrawn.' | Discussing with our child how they behave when they are feeling a particular way, 'When you are angry, how do you react?' |

**EXERCISE: COMMUNICATION CHECKLIST**

Take no more than three minutes to complete each of these questions as honestly as you can. Move on to the next question after three minutes and leave any you can't complete unanswered. Do the exercise for each of your children separately.

| 58 | How do you show your child that you are listening to him/her? |
|----|----|
| 59 | How do they show you that they are listening to you? |
| 60 | What do you like to talk about with your child? |
| 61 | What does your child like to talk to you about? |
| 62 | How do you show your child you are happy? |
| 63 | How does your child show you that he/she is happy? |
| 64 | How do you show your child you are sad or angry? |
| 65 | How does your child show you that he/she is sad or angry? |
| 66 | How did your own parents show you that they were happy or sad? |

This exercise is designed to help us reflect on the core parenting skills of listening, talking and expressing our feelings to our child. The exercise also helps us to consider how our child communicates with us, particularly regarding their emotions. The last question in this exercise asks us to explore the influence our own parents might be having on our communication skills. Our answers remind us how we communicate with our child and how we ensure our child knows we are listening to them and interested in talking to them. The answers also reinforce for us the skills we may have in communicating our emotions and helping our child communicate their emotions.

Answers we found difficult or questions we couldn't answer are important. Perhaps finding time to listen and communicate with our child is difficult for us, or perhaps we find listening and communicating difficult in general. Again, unanswered questions can suggest that we may find it difficult to communicate certain emotions or to facilitate our child to communicate his or her emotions. These unanswered questions are an opportunity for us to address these difficulties.

Teaching our child how to communicate, and in particular how to communicate emotions, is an important aspect of building their emotional welfare. Reflecting on our abilities in this area is therefore particularly important.

## Building strong self-esteem

Self-esteem is the collection of beliefs that we have about ourselves. Healthy self-esteem is a child's armour against the challenges of the world and particularly against emotional challenges. Children who believe good things about themselves have an easier time handling conflicts, resisting stress or despondency, and finding solutions to problems. In contrast, for children who have low self-esteem, challenges can become sources of major anxiety and frustration. In this way, self-esteem is one of the core influences on emotional health and parents can make a big difference to a child's self-esteem. Some of the skills involved in building our child's self-esteem are outlined in the helpsheet on the following page.

| HELP SHEET: Building Self-Esteem | | | |
|---|---|---|---|
| **Giving our child a sense of control over their own lives**<br><br>Feeling that we have control over our lives makes us feel good about ourselves. This is particularly true of children who are only learning how to control their world. | **Having reasonable and individualised expectations**<br><br>Our child will want to please and make us happy, therefore it is important that our expectations of them are reasonable and age-appropriate so that they feel they are succeeding. We can't be experts in child development but we can find out as much as possible and never expect too much from our child too early. | **Praising and reinforcing our child**<br><br>Children who are genuinely praised will have positive self-esteem. | **Being a positive role model**<br><br>Having positive self-esteem and showing this to our child helps reinforce self-esteem in them. |
| **0–4 YEARS**<br><br>Giving our child age-appropriate choices and allowing them make their own decisions, such as placing two toys in front of them and allowing them to chose which one to play with. | Learning what to generally expect from children of this age and giving our child leeway, such as recognising that temper tantrums and waking at night are normal behaviours. Allowing our child to walk, speak and be toilet-trained at their own pace and celebrating this achievement whenever it occurs. | Continually telling them they are good when they do things to deserve such praise, no matter how small. Ignoring setbacks or behaviour we don't like. This is explored more in the section on positive discipline. | Saying good things about ourselves. 'Mammy is good at fixing things'. 'Dad is good at cooking.' |
| **4–12 YEARS**<br><br>Allowing them to make more important decisions within parameters, 'What would you like for your school lunch tomorrow? You know you can choose something healthy and a treat.' | Learning what to generally expect from children of this age and giving our child leeway, such as recognising that children learn to read and do maths at different rates and some are more social than others. | Encouraging them to self-praise in an honest and modest way by guiding them. 'So you think you are good at football, I think you are as well.' | Asking them what they think we are good at. |
| **12–16 YEARS**<br><br>Talking about the key things that happened to them in their day from their perspective but focusing on how their interpretation of these events reflects how they see themselves. 'John didn't pick me for his chase team today because I'm too slow.' | Learning what to generally expect from children of this age and supporting our child to develop at their own pace while celebrating each achievement. 'I know you are finding it difficult since you started secondary school but lots of others feel the same and things will work out in time. Don't worry about your grades, they are not all that matters.' | Encouraging them to celebrate their strengths and skills, 'What do you think is your best subject … ? I agree.' | Discussing our strengths with them and acknowledging them together. |

| | | | |
|---|---|---|---|
| **16–21 YEARS** Enabling them to discuss how they see and feel about themselves and how others make them feel. Supporting them when their views are accurate and challenging them gently when they are inaccurate. | Learning what to generally expect from children of this age and giving our child leeway; celebrating their achievements whenever they occur; discussing their own expectations and helping them keep them in perspective. | Building on their self-praise by reinforcing what they think they are good at. | Asking them to support our own positive beliefs about ourselves. |

**EXERCISE: Building Self-Esteem**

Take no more than three minutes to complete each of these questions as honestly as you can. Move on to the next question after three minutes and leave any you can't complete unanswered. Do the exercise for each of your children separately.

| 67 | What is the most important decision you allow your child to make for him/herself? |
|---|---|
| 68 | What is the one thing your child does that positively surprises you? |
| 69 | What is the thing you praise your child for most? |
| 70 | What do you tell your child you are good at most often? |
| 71 | What were the most important decisions your parents let you make at the age your child is now? |
| 72 | How did you make your parents proud? |
| 73 | What did your parents praise you for most when you were your child's age? |
| 74 | What did you think your mother was particularly good at when you were a child? |
| 75 | What did you think your father was particularly good at when you were a child? |

This exercise addresses two key components of building self-esteem: our willingness and ability to trust and praise our child, and our understanding of self-esteem as gleaned from our own childhoods. Our answers to these questions reinforces for us how trusting and praising our child is an important component of building their confidence and self-esteem. The answers also remind us how our own self-esteem as children was nurtured and developed.

The questions we found difficult or could not answer give us an opportunity to assess whether we feel this is a particular area of strength for us as a parent or whether it needs more development. It also gives us an opportunity to reflect on our own childhood experiences and whether our parents were strong or weak at building our own self-esteem.

## Creating a safe, nurturing environment

A key factor influencing how our child feels about themselves concerns how safe they feel. Creating a safe environment for our child in which they feel respected and valued is important in enhancing their emotional health and psychological resilience. Physical safety is vital but emotional safety is equally as important. When they are young, children are most dependent on parents to create this sense of safety, while as they get older they can take more responsibility for this themselves.

Of course creating a safe home environment is crucial, but it is equally important to ensure that our child is safe in school and in other places they play and socialise. There is of course only so much we can do to control external risks to our child, and overprotecting them does them no good. In chapter five we discuss this in more detail; however, it is worth remembering that the best we can do is take appropriate precautions and arm our child with the skills to identify and cope with risks when they arise.

## Teaching positive discipline creates emotionally healthy children

To feel good about themselves children need to learn how to obey rules and to control their own behaviour. This involves learning to respect others, to give and take, and to make the right decisions when confronted with moral and ethical decisions. Teaching our child discipline, and particularly self-discipline, is a core function of helping them to feel good about themselves. A well-disciplined child will be more secure and more confident. Disciplining our child teaches them about right and wrong, enables them to contribute to society in a constructive way and helps them be secure, happy people.

Some parents associate discipline with punishment, such as slapping, usually because they were taught discipline through such punishments themselves. Others resort to punishment because they find their child's behaviour extremely difficult to handle or feel under pressure from family, friends or other parents. However, simply put, punishment-based discipline does not work, creates difficulties in the parent/child relationship and in many cases fosters the opposite of positive self-discipline. In addition, for most of us, punishing our child just doesn't feel right. The helpsheet on the next page gives some useful guidance on how best to teach positive discipline at different ages.

| HELP SHEET: Teaching Positive Discipline Hint Sheet | | | |
|---|---|---|---|
| **Praising and rewarding good behaviour and ignoring poor behaviour**<br>Praising behaviour we want to encourage will result in our child engaging in this behaviour. Ignored behaviour usually disappears over time. | **Having reasonable expectations about what requires discipline**<br>Our child will want to behave well and receive our praise and attention. Having reasonable expectations about what to expect from our child is important. We need to give our child leeway where possible and only focus on the most important discipline issues. | **Teaching our child about actions and consequences**<br>All actions have natural consequences and our child needs to learn this. Experiencing these consequences is an important part of learning to be disciplined. | **Being a positive role model**<br>Teaching in itself is not enough. We must practise what we preach and demonstrate self-discipline to our child ourselves. |
| **0–4 YEARS**<br>Ignore common problematic behaviour such as temper tantrums, screaming, biting; and praise enjoyable behaviour such as smiling, laughing, cuddling. | At this age our child has little sense of right or wrong, of seeing things from our perspective or of understanding fully the impact of his/her behaviour. Parents and pleasing parents is the most important thing in their life. No child at this age is trying to be bold or to annoy us. | At this age the primary way to demonstrate consequences to our child is through our actions. If our child does something dangerous we address the danger in a non-punitive, measured way. For instance, if our child cycles his bike onto the street we take the bike off him and explain it is because what he did was dangerous and we are worried about his safety. | Role modelling is particularly important at this age. Young children imitate what they see, and if, for instance, we hit out and shout, they will do the same. |
| **4–12 YEARS**<br>Ignore common problematic behaviour such as talking too much, getting upset at bedtime, fighting about having to do homework, and praise constructive behaviour such as completing homework, going to bed without a scene and sitting quietly reading and so on. | At this age our child is beginning to develop a sense of right or wrong but it is very much based on not wanting to get into trouble or displease parents, 'important' adults and teachers. There is an emerging understanding of the impact of their behaviour on others. At this age problematic behaviour usually arises from frustration and anger. | Children at this age begin to have an appreciation of our emotions if we express them clearly. Telling our child how something makes us feel in a way they can understand helps them understand the consequences of their actions. | Modelling constructive ways of dealing with our frustration will help our child learn constructive ways of dealing with their frustration, such as going into another room and distracting ourselves when we are angry. |

| | | | |
|---|---|---|---|
| **12–16 YEARS** Ignore common problematic behaviour such as not talking, being sulky and avoiding family meals, and praise constructive behaviour such as having conversations with us, no matter how brief, smiling and laughing and spending time with other family members no matter how brief. | At this age our child is only starting to fully understand the concepts of right and wrong from the perspective of others and broader society. Right and wrong is still primarily determined by the way an action makes our child feel or the impact on them. There is usually a full understanding of the impact of their behaviour on others. At this age problematic behaviour usually arises from self-centredness and self-absorption. | Discussion of consequences is very effective at this age, but in as concrete a way as possible, 'When you don't tell me what's wrong, I can't do anything to help you. When you get sulky it worries me because I think that you are unhappy.' Timing is also important. Consequences should be discussed as close to the problematic action as possible. Raising problems when our child is behaving well is not constructive; keep good times as good times. | Modelling how to express our frustrations through constructive actions and words is particularly important at this age, 'I am angry that you have not spoken to me all day so I am going to go into the sitting room for a while to calm down'. |
| **16–21 YEARS** Ignore common problematic behaviour such as being self-absorbed, coming in too late, disrespecting you, and praise constructive behaviour such as considering your feelings, speaking nicely to you and texting or phoning when asked. | At this age we should expect our child to have a good sense of right and wrong from the perspective of the greater good of society. Problematic behaviour usually arises from self-centredness, self-absorption and a disregard for others. | Abstract discussion of consequences is useful at this age, 'Taking drugs affects your ability to concentrate and can have serious consequences.' | Discussing what we do in certain situations is effective at this age, 'Sometimes when I am angry I feel like screaming but I find I calm down after having a cup of tea.' |

**EXERCISE: TEACHING POSITIVE DISCIPLINE**

Take no more than three minutes to complete each of these questions as honestly as you can. Move on to the next question after three minutes and leave any you can't complete unanswered. Do the exercise for each of your children separately.

| 76 | Which of your child's behaviours do you praise the most? |
|----|----------------------------------------------------------|
| 77 | Which of his/her behaviours do you ignore the most? |
| 78 | What one of his/her behaviours positively surprises you most? |
| 79 | What does he/she do that particularly pleases you? |
| 80 | What has he/she done recently that you feel has taught them something positive about being disciplined? |
| 81 | What has he/she done recently that you feel has taught them something negative about being disciplined? |
| 82 | What do you do to model positive discipline for your child? |
| 83 | What is your most positive self-discipline strength? |
| 84 | What one good thing did your own parents teach you about discipline? |

The purpose of this exercise is to help us reflect on how we foster positive discipline in our child and how we model positive discipline. The questions are designed to help us focus on the use of praise, our discipline techniques and the key skill of ignoring negative behaviour. The last question in this exercise helps us to consider what we might have carried from our own childhoods regarding discipline. The emphasis in the exercise is on learning as an important ongoing component of discipline. Our answers remind us of our skills in this area and of the self-discipline our child is beginning to develop. The answers can also reinforce for us our own self-discipline, what influences this and how important this is as modelling for our child.

Reflecting on the questions we found difficult or could not answer is also important. These might suggest that we are having difficulty teaching our child discipline or that we find it difficult to be self-disciplined ourselves at times. This might require us to give some more thought to this area or may provide the impetus for us to begin to start developing our skills and insights.

Positive discipline is an important component of our child feeling secure and good about themselves. Teaching this skill to our child is important and is made easier if we have already developed some positive self-discipline skills ourselves.

## Teaching spiritual and/or philosophical beliefs

To feel good about themselves, people need to feel that there is a greater purpose to life than just their everyday existence. Believing in a greater purpose is an important part of feeling good about ourselves. It helps to motivate us and to make sense of adversity and sadness when we experience it. For younger children, understanding abstract concepts can be difficult and so teaching about beliefs must be concrete and easy to grasp. As they get older they develop the ability to understand more abstract concepts.

Just as a child needs to develop physically and emotionally, they also need to develop spiritually and/or philosophically. Preaching our own beliefs in a dogmatic way does not help. Helping our child understand and learn about what we believe in, while allowing them the space to explore and develop their own beliefs at an age-appropriate level, is important. Allowing time for our child to ask questions and answering them honestly is also important.

Just as with other aspects of their development, we cannot determine our child's spiritual or philosophical beliefs. We can, however, work hard to try to ensure they do develop beliefs and that these give them an optimistic outlook on life.

| **EXERCISE:** TEACHING SPIRITUAL AND PHILOSOPHICAL BELIEFS |
|---|
| Take no more than three minutes to complete each of these questions as honestly as you can. Move on to the next question after three minutes and leave any you can't complete unanswered. Do the exercise for each of your children separately. |

| 85 | What one spiritual/philosophical activity do you do with your child? |
|---|---|
| 86 | What one spiritual/philosophical thing do you talk about with your child? |
| 87 | What one spiritual/philosophical thing do you remember doing with your own parents? |
| 88 | What one spiritual/philosophical thing do you remember talking about with your own parents? |
| 89 | What is the one most important spiritual/philosophical belief you would like your child to have? |
| 90 | What is the one most important spiritual/philosophical belief your parents taught you? |

This exercise is designed to help us reflect on the importance of teaching spiritual and philosophical beliefs to our child. The exercise emphasises the importance of teaching these beliefs through both actions and words. The last question in the exercise addresses the issue of what we have carried with us from our own childhoods. Our answers give us insight into how we are helping our child develop belief systems in this area.

Difficulty in answering some questions may indicate that we have not given this aspect of parenting much thought and that we need to consider developing it further. Having good emotional health requires our child to have developed spiritual and philosophical beliefs. This helps them give meaning to their world and to better deal with challenges and traumas when they arise. For parents it is difficult to help our child develop such beliefs if we have not developed them ourselves or have not given the matter adequate consideration. This exercise is designed to help us reflect and grow in this area.

## Summary

Teaching a child self-belief is an essential part of helping them develop emotional health and psychological resilience. Feeling good about themselves does not mean that they believe that they are perfect or are better than others. It is, rather, teaching them the ability to recognise and appreciate their own strengths and weaknesses and their distinct set of personality traits, skills and abilities. Helping them to foster self-belief and how to feel good about themselves also encourages them to see the good in others.

# four

## Meeting Emotional Health Challenges

'Yes I have seen lots of children whose lives have become just that bit too much for them. They have withdrawn. You can see the sadness and worry in their eyes. But when you looked hard enough there was in every one that potential to be happy and to enjoy life. It just needed to be unlocked.'

Raising emotionally healthy children involves connecting with our inner parent and teaching our child how to be happy and how to feel good about themselves. Being emotionally healthy not only protects our child from developing emotional difficulties but also helps them deal with difficulties if they do arise.

However, no matter how emotionally healthy our child is, they can experience emotional difficulties. If this happens, the important thing to remember is that this is quite normal and can be managed. Most, if not all, emotional difficulties are manageable if the right supports are made available.

### What are emotional difficulties?

As we know from previous chapters, emotional health is best described in the context of feelings and actions. When we are emotionally healthy we feel generally happy, content and confident, and we engage in mainly positive, enjoyable actions and activities. When we are emotionally unhealthy we feel sad, angry, discontented and detached for a disproportionate amount of time, sometimes for no apparent reason. Moreover we engage in predominantly negative actions and activities towards ourselves and/or others. Few of us are completely emotionally healthy all of the time, and few are completely unhealthy all of the time. The line or boundary between being emotionally healthy and unhealthy is often difficult to define and can be different for different people. There are many sublevels of being healthy or unhealthy.

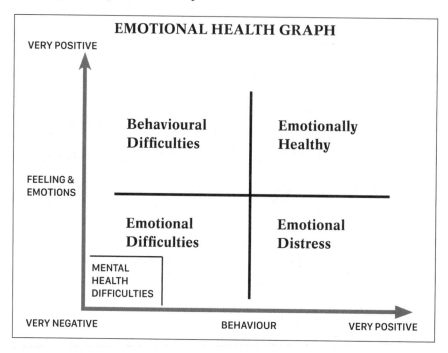

**EMOTIONAL HEALTH GRAPH**

VERY POSITIVE

FEELING & EMOTIONS

**Behavioural Difficulties**

**Emotionally Healthy**

**Emotional Difficulties**

**Emotional Distress**

MENTAL HEALTH DIFFICULTIES

VERY NEGATIVE    BEHAVIOUR    VERY POSITIVE

## Why is it important to be emotionally healthy?

Being emotionally healthy not only makes us happier and more content but also better equips us to deal with the challenges that life presents. For children, being emotionally healthy gives them the best chance of having a happy childhood and of growing and developing to the best of their potential.

## Why do emotional difficulties occur?

Emotional difficulties are usually caused by a combination of three factors: a child's personality; the type of experiences a child has; and the type of supports available to a child.

## Personality

As we discussed in chapter three, children are born with their own unique personalities and this is particularly apparent in their emotional and psychological characteristics. Some children are born with a biological or neurological makeup that makes them more prone to worry or sadness than others. Some like physical contact while others may not. Some withdraw from distress and upset while others engage completely, demonstrating their distress overtly. Our child's personality provides the hard drive on which their future emotional health and psychological characteristics are built. While this hard drive might be predetermined, how it develops is not. Parents play an important role in shaping how the components of a child's personality develop and emerge, and in particular how it impacts on their emotional health. A child's experiences and the support he/she receives also shapes how their personality develops.

A child's personality is rarely the sole cause of the emergence of emotional difficulties, but there is little doubt that in most children their personalities play a part. For instance, two siblings in the company of their mother witnessing a car accident may have very different psychological reactions to what they see even if they receive the same support from their mother.

## Experiences

Happy, enjoyable and rewarding experiences make people emotionally stronger, while traumatic and upsetting experiences make them emotionally weaker. This is particularly true of children who are only learning to cope with challenges and whose emotional personalities are only beginning to be fully formed. Protecting our children from as many stressful or sad experiences as possible for as long as possible makes them emotionally stronger. Negative experiences contribute significantly to the emergence of emotional difficulties, although no matter how traumatic or upsetting the experience, it is rarely the sole cause of a difficulty.

Of course we can't completely protect our child from negative experiences but we can, where possible, limit their unnecessary exposure to them. We can also try to shape and support their responses to these experiences to lessen the psychological impact. Our child will interpret their experiences in their own unique way and we need to appreciate and be sensitive to this. For instance, we cannot protect our child from experiencing the death of a loved one, but we can and should protect them from being bullied. Their responses to both occurrences will be unique to themselves.

**Supports**

As we know, children cope better with stress and sadness if they have good emotional supports. Emotional support means giving space and confidence to our child to allow them to speak about and discuss their problems and negative feelings. They need to be able to do this in the knowledge that their feelings will be taken seriously and their views will be the most important factor in deciding how difficulties are interpreted and managed.

Support for children from us, their parents, is crucial; however, supports from siblings, peers and other trusted adults, such as teachers, should not be underestimated. Sometimes the best we as parents can do is to sit back and allow others provide the support our child needs.

While good supports can help alleviate even the most traumatic life experiences, lack of support, particularly for emotionally sensitive children, can contribute significantly to the emergence of emotional difficulties. For instance, a sensitive child who is bullied but who has strong parental and peer support is unlikely to develop problems, whereas without strong supports the emergence of difficulties is highly likely.

How these three factors combine is still the subject of much study and debate. From a parenting perspective it is best to consider that each plays an equal role in influencing our child's emotional health. The impact of each can be alleviated by the others and at different times in our child's life any one of these factors can be the strongest determinant.

## General indicators of emotional difficulties in children

If our child starts to experience emotional difficulties, he/she will demonstrate this through their behaviour, communication and feelings. Such emotional difficulties usually involve our child becoming overly anxious or worried, or becoming overly sad and depressed.

If our child becomes overly anxious we will most likely notice them starting to have extreme, unrealistic worries about everyday activities. This may occur in lots of different situations and in lots of different ways. Our child might start to have difficulty leaving us to go to playschool or school. They might refuse to participate in the hobbies they usually enjoy or appear reluctant to visit a relative or friend's house. They might start to develop unrealistic and excessive fears about certain situations or objects such as animals or storms. Physical signs of anxiety such as pounding heartbeat, sweating, dizziness, nausea or a feeling that they think they are going to die, are common. They might start to have the same thoughts and to repeat the same behaviours continuously, and if they have had a particularly stressful event in their lives they might have strong memories and flashbacks of this event.

If our child is experiencing anxiety they will usually complain of physical problems like stomach aches and headaches, which, on further investigation, do not have any physical cause. As a result there may be frequent visits to the doctor or school absences. When our child is experiencing anxiety they will usually become self-conscious and may feel teachers or their friends are talking about them.

If our child starts to become sad or depressed we will most likely start to notice them being frequently tearful or sad while withdrawing from friends or from normal daily activities. They will seem to have no enthusiasm or motivation to do anything and will lack any energy. Their eating and sleep may become disrupted. They will sleep too much during the day and wake at night. As a result of this they will be more agitated and aggressive. This aggression will be most evident in their play. They will refuse to eat at meal times or eat excessively.

In younger children depression can sometimes present itself as boldness and uncooperativeness. In older children sadness and depression will most likely manifest themselves in recurring thoughts and conversations about death and their drawings and paintings might become darker. They will express feelings of guilt and hopelessness and will be very sensitive to rejection or failure. They will appear to see themselves as worthless and sometimes engage in self-harm.

The younger or less mature our child, the more likely they are to express emotional difficulties through their behaviour. The table on the next page outlines some of the main ways that emotional difficulties can start to emerge at different ages. It is important to remember that many of these indicators commonly arise with most children from time to time. It is only when they occur for no apparent reason, are out of character with our child, or persist despite our support and intervention that we should begin to consider the possibility of emotional difficulties. We know our child best so if our instinct tells us something is not right we should pay attention to this.

## HELP SHEET: Indicators of Emotional Difficulties

| | Behaviour | Communication | Emotion |
|---|---|---|---|
| **0–4 YEARS** | Overly clingy<br><br>Speech delay<br><br>Starting to bed wet/soil again having been toilet-trained<br><br>Refusing to eat<br><br>Inappropriate play<br><br>Over-attachment to strangers<br><br>Waking through the night upset | Frequent expressions of unhappiness and dissatisfaction for no apparent reason<br><br>Saying they don't like things for no apparent reason<br><br>Shouting, screaming or being scared or frightened for no apparent reason | Crying for no apparent reason<br><br>Showing no emotion and becoming withdrawn<br><br>Breaking toys aggressively<br><br>Deliberately hurting siblings, parents or friends |
| **5–12 YEARS** | Refusing to go to school<br><br>Sitting in front of the television for long periods<br><br>Showing no interest in seeing friends<br><br>Overly checking homework, possessions, their room<br><br>Being overly clingy<br><br>Being aggressive with friends, parents or adults<br><br>Continually moving around, picking things up, fidgeting, breaking things<br><br>Waking at night for no reason<br><br>Low energy levels<br><br>Eating too much or too little<br><br>Sleep disturbance<br><br>Inability to control behaviour<br><br>Getting into trouble in school<br><br>Withdrawing from friends | Refusing to speak<br><br>Speaking aggressively to siblings, parents, friends or teachers<br><br>Shouting/screaming<br><br>Speaking about things that don't make any sense to us<br><br>Telling lies that are certain to be found out<br><br>Constantly needing reassurance<br><br>Constantly talking about sad, ugly things<br><br>Saying they are worried with no apparent cause | Crying for no apparent reason<br><br>Getting upset for no apparent reason when with friends<br><br>Worrying unduly<br><br>Frequent sadness<br><br>Lack of enthusiasm<br><br>Erratic emotions |
| **13–21 YEARS** | Sleeping too much during the day and too little at night<br><br>Misusing alcohol or drugs<br><br>Self-harm<br><br>Withdrawal from activities they enjoyed in the past<br><br>Spending too much time in their bedroom or on the computer<br><br>Deterioration of personal hygiene<br><br>Failure to attend school or college<br><br>Fretting over minor tasks and fixating on where their possessions are<br><br>Never being satisfied that they have everything they need or have done enough work<br><br>Spending too much time on tasks | Saying hurtful things to friends or parents for no apparent reason<br><br>Expressing feelings of hopelessness/despair<br><br>Preoccupation with talking about sad things or death<br><br>Preoccupation with talking about stressful things<br><br>Saying they would prefer if they were dead | Preoccupation with talking about stressful things<br><br>Saying they would prefer if they were dead<br><br>Crying for no apparent reason<br><br>Getting upset for no apparent reason when with friends<br><br>Worrying unduly<br><br>Frequent sadness<br><br>Lack of enthusiasm<br><br>Erratic emotions<br><br>Inability to concentrate<br><br>Lack of energy |

**EXERCISE: CHILD EMOTIONAL DIFFICULTIES**

Take no more than three minutes to complete each of these questions as honestly as you can. Answer yes or no to each question. Do the exercise for each of your children separately. Base your answers on what has occurred over the last two weeks.

- Has your child begun to start acting like they did when they were younger or started to have toileting problems?

- Does your child worry excessively about a number of events or activities?

- Does your child experience shortness of breath or a racing heart for no apparent reason?

- Does your child find it difficult to interact with family members and other familiar people and to get enjoyment from these interactions?

- Does your child often appear anxious when interacting with friends, or does he/she try to avoid them?

- Does your child have a persistent and unreasonable fear of an object or situation, such as flying, heights or animals? When encountering the feared object or situation, does he/she react by freezing, clinging or having a tantrum?

- Does your child worry excessively about their abilities and how others view them?

- Does your child cry, have tantrums or refuse to leave a family member when necessary?

- Has your child started to refuse to go to day care or school, experienced a decline in school performance or started to avoid other age-appropriate social activities?

- Does your child spend at least one hour each day repeating things over again, such as hand washing, checking, arranging or counting?

- Does your child have exaggerated and irrational fears of people, places, objects or situations that interfere with their social and academic life?

- Does your child experience many nightmares, headaches or stomach aches?

- Does your child repetitively use toys to re-enact scenes from a disturbing event?

- Does your child redo tasks because of excessive dissatisfaction with less-than-perfect performance?

- Does your child have or express little interest or pleasure in doing things?

- Does your child seem or say that he/she is feeling down, depressed or hopeless?

- Does your child have, or say they have, trouble falling or staying asleep, or are they sleeping too much?

- Does your child seem or say that they feel tired or have little energy?

- Does your child have a poor appetite or do they overeat?

- Does your child say that he/she feels bad about themselves or that they are a failure or have let themselves or your family down?

- Does your child have trouble concentrating on things such as reading or watching television?

- Does your child move or speak so slowly that other people have noticed?

- Is your child fidgety or restless or have they been moving around a lot more than usual?

- Has your child expressed thoughts that they would be better off dead or of hurting themselves in some way?

This exercise is designed to help you to reflect on behaviours or feelings which could suggest that your child is experiencing emotional difficulties. The first set of questions focuses on indicators which are often associated with children who are experiencing stress and anxiety, while the second set focus on indicators which are related to depression. It is useful to consider each of the questions you answered yes to by asking yourself if this behaviour or feeling is out of character for your child and if there is something happening in your child's life which explains them. If you are particularly concerned about any of the ones you answered yes to, or if you answered yes to more than four questions, it would be useful to discuss these issues with your child directly. If, after discussing them with your child, you still remain concerned, it would be useful to discuss the matter with the school or to ask your doctor to direct you to appropriate supports.

## What is the impact of emotional difficulties?

Emotional difficulties not only cause our child to be unhappy but can, if they become too dominant, impact on our child's ability to function normally. The impact on our children can be particularly severe because of their developmental vulnerabilities. Aside from the emotional effects of unhappiness and distress that arise, the social effects such as missing school and withdrawing from friends, can be equally as harmful.

## What do I do if I discover my child is having emotional difficulties?

Childhood emotional difficulties are not uncommon and can be managed and resolved effectively if we follow a small number of important principles. These are best described as the Seven Ss.

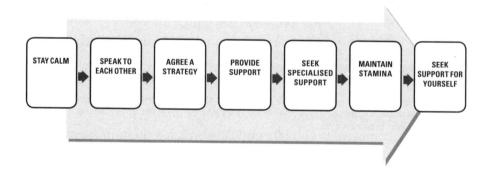

S1. STAY CALM: The first thing that we need to do if we believe or become worried that our child might be experiencing emotional difficulties is to stay calm. While some level of panic and upset is likely it is very important that we take control of our feelings and keep our thoughts in perspective.

S2. SPEAK TO EACH OTHER: It is imperative that we discuss our concerns with our child directly, no matter what age they are. It is often difficult to distinguish emotional difficulties from the normal mood swings of growing up. Therefore, the second important step to take if we become concerned that our child is having problems is to explore with him/her how they feel and why they think they feel this way. This is also the quickest and easiest way to find out how severe the difficulties might be.

Sometimes parents worry that discussing such issues will only make their child more upset and distressed. Our child might at first be reluctant to discuss their difficulties out of embarrassment. However, in the end they will be relieved to be able to tell somebody how they are really feeling. It is important to engage in this conversation at an appropriate level for our child, using terms they understand and trying our best to understand what they are telling us in their own way. They will most likely not have developed the capacity to understand or describe their emotions in detail as yet. It is up to us as parents to try and interpret and understand what they are trying to tell us or might mean without imposing our own beliefs or worries on them. The following tips are useful to keep in mind:

- Keep the conversation as practical and straightforward as possible: 'I notice you seem sad right now; are you?'
- Ask open-ended questions: 'can you tell me what is making you sad?'
- Take the lead from your child's answers and try to use the language and words your child uses: 'so you feel bad; what do you think is making you feel this way?'
- Try to put meaning on your child's words for them in ways that they will understand and by checking with them that you are getting it right: 'when you feel bad do you feel like crying and not talking? Is this right?'

- Show as much understanding as possible and avoid confrontation or disagreement: 'I know it is not nice to feel bad, so let's try to see what might help?'

S3. AGREE A STRATEGY: Emotional difficulties are best approached in the same way as we would approach any other problem or difficulty we encounter in life, by forming a plan or a strategy. We need to try to agree, with our child, what might help the situation. We cannot expect our child to know exactly what might help as if they knew they would be taking these actions already. However they will have some idea as to what might help and we need to guide them towards other options.

Sometimes the options might seem frightening for our child at first so we need to fully understand what they involve and we need to gently explain the benefits to them. In some very rare situations where a child is very distressed or experiencing severe difficulties it might be necessary for us to take actions that they do not agree with. This should only be done where we feel our child's needs outweigh the requirement for agreement or where we believe they are too distressed to be able to agree. For instance, our child says he is being bullied in school and this is causing him immense distress but he is pleading with us not to talk to his teacher or to the parents of the children doing the bullying. To protect our child and help him resolve his emotional difficulties it might be necessary for us to address the bullying without his/her agreement but ideally with their knowledge.

S4. PROVIDE SUPPORT: If we believe our child is experiencing emotional difficulties it is imperative that we provide them with support and seek support for ourselves. The most important support we can provide to our child comes from us and involves the following:

- *Recognising that their distress is real:* This involves empathising with our child and allowing them to openly express their feelings without judging or dismissing them, no matter how unreasonable or trivial they might seem to us. One of the hardest things for a person to do is to try to fully understand the cause and the resultant feelings of an emotional difficulty. Our first inclination is to suggest solutions, minimise the feelings or dismiss them as unreasonable. Being able to talk about their distress without feeling judged will help our child.

- *Reinforcing how much we love them and care for them:* We cannot tell our child we love and care for them enough. This is particularly true when they are distressed. Expressing this makes them feel more secure and willing to talk openly about how they feel. Sometimes these sentiments are enough to help them overcome specific difficulties that might be causing them some distress. Where difficulties are more engrained, these sentiments in themselves won't resolve things but they will help our child and us find the best way to access alternative solutions.

- *Reinforcing emotional health and psychological resilience skills:* No matter how upset or distressed our child is, reinforcing the emotional health and psychological resilience skills discussed in chapters two and three will benefit them and in many cases will resolve the distress and difficulties they are experiencing. Even when our child is acutely distressed and needs additional help these skills will benefit them in the long term by speeding the resolution of their problems and reducing the chances of them reoccurring.

- *Teaching them basic emotional distress management skills:* These skills include supporting and teaching them how to rate, confront and rationalise anxieties, relaxation and mindfulness skills, the skills of positive thinking. They also involve teaching them the skills of recognising the early signs of emotional difficulties. We don't have to be experts in any of these skills ourselves to be able to provide our child with the basics. The important thing is to find skills that they and we can relate to easily.

- *Addressing things in our child's environment:* In chapter five we discuss how creating an emotionally healthy and safe environment is crucial for our child's emotional health. When difficulties arise it is important to assess if there is anything in our child's environment that might be causing or exacerbating their difficulties. Common factors might be bullying in school, isolation from other children, difficulties at home. Addressing these factors alone may resolve a child's difficulties, but even if they don't it will certainly reduce the distress.

S5. SEEK SPECIALISED SUPPORT: Sometimes no matter how much support we provide to our child their emotional difficulties are too severe and too engrained and we need to access specialised help. If this occurs we firstly need to remember the first S and stay calm. Many children require specialised help and the research indicates that with the right type of help children can overcome their difficulties and live good, enjoyable lives.

The type of specialised support best suited to our child will be determined by the type of difficulties our child is experiencing, our child's personality and the other supports our child has in their lives. To help us access the right option it is best to consult our family doctor. He/she will be able to provide an initial assessment of our child's needs and to recommend the most appropriate steps. There will also be support systems attached to our child's school so it can be useful to access these by talking to our child's teacher.

*Talking Therapies:* Research has established that talking therapies are very effective for supporting children with a variety of emotional difficulties. There are numerous different types but the most commonly used is cognitive behavioural therapy. These therapies focus on our child's thinking and behaviour and are based on the principle that changing these will improve our child's emotional health. With younger children, play and sensory therapies are very effective ways of helping them resolve emotional difficulties. For most children, talking therapies are effective and also arm them with techniques they can use in the future if further difficulties arise.

The important thing to remember about talking therapies is that the therapist and the therapist's relationship with our child are crucial to the effectiveness of the therapy. It is therefore essential that we access this type of support from a qualified, experienced therapist and we obtain a therapist who fits with or gets on with our child, no matter how long this takes and no matter how many therapists this requires seeing. Assessing the suitability of the therapist involves us exploring with them what service they provide and how they work before committing our child to their care. It also involves finding out more about them from trusted sources such as our child's school or our family doctor. Many different professionals provide talking therapies but the best form is provided as part of a team of professionals and as part of a cohesive treatment or care plan.

*Making Life Changes:* To address a child's emotional difficulties, life changes are usually required. Sometimes making such changes can be the most effective way of addressing our child's difficulties. If there are particular life circumstances that are causing a child to be stressed or depressed and they can be addressed then they should be.

Even if a child requires talking therapy it will be less effective if the issues causing particular difficulty are not addressed. In chapter five we deal in more detail with creating emotionally healthy environments for children.

*Medication:* In some cases a child may require medication to help them through particularly stressful or depressing periods. The decision to use medication should never be taken lightly and needs to be given careful consideration when it comes to children. Nonetheless for some difficulties and for some children medication, in conjunction with talk therapy, is the most effective.

The assessment of the need for medication is usually informed by multiple variables, including the severity of symptoms a child is experiencing, the adverse impact on a child's life caused by their difficulties and a child's previous response to medication. The standard medications used to treat childhood emotional difficulties are not habit forming or addictive. These medications do not usually change personalities but are used to treat the symptoms with the aim of helping the young person feel like himself or herself again.

S6. MAINTAIN STAMINA: Addressing emotional difficulties takes time, so it is important that both parent and child maintain energy and engagement. Because difficulties affect both behaviour and feelings, resolution of them is rarely straightforward. Key to maintaining our stamina is remembering that overcoming difficulties is not only possible but is to be expected. Resolving difficulties is not likely to be straightforward. Sometimes there are setbacks and sometimes it takes longer than we expect.

We all have our own very personal views and beliefs about emotional health and emotional difficulties. There are many misconceptions, which no matter how hard we try to resist, can influence our thinking. For example some people feel that emotional difficulties are not treatable and will inevitably become serious mental health difficulties that a person never recovers from. Others believe that emotional difficulties result from personality weaknesses which are unchangeable, while others believe that they are reflective of poor parenting and social deprivation. These beliefs are particularly damaging to children.

If our child's emotional difficulties continue for any length of time these misconceptions can come to the fore. Sometimes we lose hope and begin to feel our child will never recover. At other times we can get angry with our child and feel they should do more to 'pull themselves together'. We might begin to blame ourselves and feel ashamed or guilty that our child has these difficulties and feel that in some way we are responsible or have let them down. These are all natural feelings that stem from our distress. At these times it is important that we refocus ourselves on the reality that any child can experience emotional difficulties and that our child will resolve these difficulties if we remain positive and hopeful. Focusing on the positive aspects of our child's life and what is going well for them is crucial. Even at times of distress this will help them and us move forward.

S7. SEEK SUPPORT FOR OURSELVES: Seeing our child in distress will inevitably cause us distress. Supporting and helping them can cause us to become even more stressed, downhearted and hopeless. While doing all we can for our child we must also ensure we protect our own emotional health. If we don't we cannot be of any real help to our child. This might require us seeking extra support for ourselves. Looking after ourselves is explored in more detail in chapter six.

**How can a reoccurrence of emotional difficulties be prevented?**
When our child begins feeling positive after an episode of emotional difficulty we should feel happy and proud of them and of ourselves. This is a time to celebrate their achievement and to take the opportunity to

live and enjoy life. Reinforcing all of the actions identified in chapters two to five is important. It is also a good time to put an Individual Emotional Health Enhancement Plan (IEHEP) in place with our child. An IEHEP has four components:

1. *Developing an emotional health toolbox with our child:* This is a list of skills, techniques or actions our child can use to stay emotionally healthy. Ideally these should be skills they already have but the list can also contain things we would like to teach or encourage our child to engage in.

2. *Outlining a daily emotional health plan:* This involves timetabling things into our child's day which we know will relax them and give them enjoyment. No matter what occurs in the day our child is given the opportunity to do these things.

3. *Identifying triggers and early warning signs and structuring a plan to deal with these:* This involves agreeing with our child what signs and symptoms we should be watchful for and what are good positive signs.

4. *Agreeing an action plan for relapses:* This is a plan we agree with our child when they are well that should be followed if they become unwell again.

The following is an example of an IEHEP for a twelve-year-old child called Robert who developed anxiety difficulties which caused him to miss a great deal of school. He complained to the doctor of frequent stomach aches and began to lose contact with his friends. He attended the school counsellor for three months and is now progressing well.

**ROBERT'S INDIVIDUAL EMOTIONAL HEALTH ENHANCEMENT PLAN**

| Emotional Health Toolbox | I will practise the relaxation, mindfulness skills I learned and am good at once every two days. | I will chat with my mum or dad each evening about my main worries and about the things I enjoyed during the day. | I will practice focusing on the thoughts that make me feel good. | I will write down the main things in my head (worries and tasks) on a piece of paper before going to sleep every night. |
|---|---|---|---|---|
| Daily emotional health plan | I will spend thirty minutes every day playing sport. | I will spend thirty minutes every day reading a leisure book of my choice. | I will spend thirty minutes every day with or talking to friends. | I will spend thirty minutes each day watching my favourite TV programmes. |
| Triggers and early signs | If I start checking and rechecking that I have all the right books in my bag before going to school, resulting in me leaving the house late. | If I can't sleep at night worrying whether I have all of my homework completed correctly or not. | If I resume spending hours doing my homework, often tearing up pages and starting again because of small mistakes. | If I start trying to avoid going to school because I am not prepared enough or worrying I might not be able to understand the day's lessons. |
| Action plan | Put the relaxation and mindfulness techniques into practice twice a day. | Put the thought restructuring techniques I have learnt into practice. | Talk to my mum or dad each evening about my worries and listen to what they are saying about how I might be able to cope with them. | Contact the school counsellor and attend for a refresher session. |

Of course, developing an IEHEP can be a useful technique for a child to develop as an emotionally healthy living tool even if they have not experienced emotional difficulties.

## Mental health difficulties

Some children develop serious mental health difficulties that do require specialised help. When such difficulties arise it is essential to apply the seven key principles discussed previously, remembering that no matter how severe a difficulty is it can be treated and our child can continue to live a happy and enjoyable life. While detailed discussion of the types of difficulties that can arise are beyond the scope of this book, more resources for understanding and dealing with such difficulties are referenced at the back of this book. (www.mayoclinic.org and www.reachout.ie are both very useful.)

## Summary

To live life fully, children must experience stress, sadness and anger. They also need to have an imaginary life and at times to withdraw into themselves for periods, particularly if they are experiencing difficulties. When these behaviours or emotions start to occur very frequently or begin to occur to the extent that they impede upon a child's ability to live a normal, happy life, then they are starting to experience emotional difficulties.

No matter how much work we put into building our child's emotional health and psychological resilience, it is possible that they will experience some emotional difficulties at some stage in their childhood if not in their adult lives. When this occurs we need to react in the knowledge that these difficulties can be managed successfully and our child can live a good and enjoyable life. Keeping this in mind will help us to take the appropriate steps, in partnership with our child, to address the difficulties and to reduce the risk of reoccurrence.

# five

## Creating an Emotionally Healthy Environment

'As parents we spend a great deal of time worrying about our children and alcohol, drugs, bullying, abuse and damaging internet material. It can be hard for us to remember that the world we worry about as a parent is not the world our children know or experience. They, while aware of all of the dangers and risks, are more empowered, more resilient and have more choice than young people have ever had before. From this we should take heart.'

As we discussed in chapters three and four, one of the key determinants of emotional and psychological health is the environment our child lives in and their life experiences. Research the world over indicates that the more positive a child's experiences and environment the stronger they become psychologically. Positive environments and experiences also serve to outweigh the impact of negative ones.

A child's home, childcare, school and social environments will all have an impact on their emotional and psychological health. Their interactions with and usage of the internet has also become increasingly more important.

Parents of course, cannot fully control their child's experiences or all of the environments they are exposed to and if we try to, we run the risk of smothering them with too much control and risk aversion. We can, however, do all that is practical and reasonable to reduce the number of unnecessary adverse experiences our child has, particularly the younger they are. The real parenting skill in this regard is knowing how to get the right balance. Creating safe environments and positive experiences for our child takes planning and time. It also involves taking reasonable risks.

## Creating an emotionally healthy home environment

Feeling happy and supported at home is vital to a child's emotional health. A child needs a place to feel safe and free from the threats, difficulties and challenges they will encounter in their daily lives. They also need a place where they can re-energise themselves for futures activities. Their home is the place that best provides this.

Because children spend so much time with their family it is with them that they have some of the happiest, most enjoyable experiences of their childhoods. How the members of their family view them plays a key role in determining their self-esteem and self-confidence. We know from our own childhoods and experience of being parented just how important families are.

A child defines who their family is to them. Many family structures are diverse and contain fathers, stepfathers, grandparents or estranged partners and so on. Once a child defines a person as being 'family', this confers additional responsibility on that individual. A child, by defining a person as family, is indicating that he or she has made a decision to love and trust this person implicitly and to see their relationship with them as special. This makes this relationship very important to the child's emotional and psychological health.

There are many different characteristics that make a family 'emotionally healthy', but the most important are:

- Mutual respect between all family members;
- Positive communication between family members;
- Good problem-solving techniques within the family to resolve family issues;
- Good emotional awareness and expression within the family;
- An ability for family members to look introspectively at how the family is functioning.

| HELP SHEET: Creating an Emotionally Healthy Family | | | | |
|---|---|---|---|---|
| **Mutual respect** <br><br> A key component contributing to the emotional health of a family is how much respect members of the family have for each other. It is important that a child is respected within a family, that he/she sees others respecting each other and that the child himself respects others in the family. This involves ensuring all family members' privacy; wishes and choices are respected in an age-appropriate manner. A child respected in the family will develop strong self-respect. | **Positive family communication** <br><br> Communication is the energy that fuels the functioning of the family. While people can live together under the same roof, it is the communication between them that defines them as a family. | **Strong problem-solving skills** <br><br> Within families there will always be conflict. It is a natural part of resolving individual needs and wishes, but how a family resolves conflict will impact significantly on the emotional and psychological welfare of a child. | **Ability of a family to understand and deal with feelings** <br><br> How families understand and deal with feelings has an important influence on how a child learns to deal with emotions. A child will prosper emotionally within a family that has the ability to understand and constructively express feelings. | **Family introspection and awareness** <br><br> A family's ability to look at how it is functioning has the best chance of being emotionally healthy. Most families do this through everyday challenge and reinforcement. |
| **0–4 YEARS** <br><br> Allowing all family members to make age-appropriate decisions, regarding when they are touched, kissed or hugged, and what they play. | Working to ensure all family members try to listen and understand each other in an age-appropriate way. For instance, seeing younger children's behaviour as an expression of feelings and using language that is understandable to a child. | Encouraging all family members to find practical solutions to difficulties, particularly emotional ones, at an age-appropriate level. | Encouraging family members to show appropriate physical emotion such as hugging and holding hands. | Talking about and reinforcing the healthy aspects of the family. 'Going to the playground makes us all happy.' |
| **5–12 YEARS** <br><br> Ensuring all family members are talked to and not talked at. Ensuring all family members are given the opportunity to express their opinions in an age-appropriate way and these are heard and considered within the family. | Integrating communication into our everyday family activities, such as talking while eating, chatting while doing family chores. Ensuring all family members are encouraged to use age-appropriate and understandable language. | Encouraging the importance of fairness and understanding of other people's views and feelings. | Finding a common emotional language that all family members can use and understand, such as using the same term to describe being upset. Finding a healthy way to react to each other's emotions, not responding to anger with anger, not taking criticism personally. | Allowing and acting on constructive criticism of the family 'I wish we went to the cinema more together', and not becoming defensive. |

| | | | | | |
|---|---|---|---|---|---|
| **13–16 YEARS** | Respecting all family members' privacy, such as not letting others take or use their possessions without agreement, not checking their phone messages without permission. | Encouraging open, non-judgemental conversation and expression of views and opinions. | Encouraging the thinking out of decisions, particularly emotional ones, and supporting consistency of decision-making. | Challenging emotions or expressions of emotions that are unreasonable, such as allowing anger but not accepting banging doors or throwing things. Working to help each other understand the source of our emotions. | Talking openly within the family about its strengths and weaknesses, without judgement or recrimination if possible. Working to improve the unhealthy components of the family. |
| **17–21 YEARS** | Giving all family members real choices. Helping all family members to make decisions for themselves. | Supporting and encouraging the development of compromise and negotiation skills within the family. | Encouraging open, non-judgemental conversation and expression of views and opinions. | Being open about feelings by encouraging all family members to discuss them in an appropriate way. | Getting all family members to commit to working for the family and adapting to change, such as talking and agreeing regularly on practical changes that have occurred and what their emotional impact might be. |

## EXERCISE: CREATING AN EMOTIONALLY HEALTHY FAMILY

Take no more than three minutes to complete each of these questions as honestly as you can. Move on to the next question after three minutes and leave any you can't complete unanswered. Do the exercise for your family as a whole.

| 91 | Name one way that the members of your family respect each other? |
|---|---|
| 92 | What is the most effective way your family communicates with each other? |
| 93 | What solution to a problem did your family agree to this week? |
| 94 | What one emotional issue did your family deal well with this week? |
| 95 | What one thing did you learn about your family this week? |
| 96 | What one thing made you proud of your family this week? |

| 97 | What one thing has your family decided to change this week? |
|---|---|
|  |  |

This exercise asks us to reflect on how our family communicates and resolves problems and how the members of the family respect each other. Each of the questions is designed to focus on a positive aspect of family functioning. Our answers can reinforce for us the emotional strengths of our family and how that can serve to support each individual member. Questions we found difficult or could not answer suggest that this may be something we have not considered adequately, or is an aspect of our family that needs development.

The exercise recognises that change and learning are a core component of family functioning and if we found answering the questions relating to this particular aspect of family life difficult, perhaps it indicates that our family find reflection and learning difficult.

For our child's emotional well-being it is important that our family functions healthily. This exercise is designed to reinforce the positive aspects of our family functioning and to give us the incentive and direction to address the weaknesses.

## Creating an emotionally healthy child-care environment

For most parents, finding somebody to care for our child while we work is not easy. Most crèche and day-care facilities are expensive and it is hard to know how to distinguish the good ones from the bad. Finding a child-minder is also difficult and, again, it is very hard to assess how good or bad they might be. Choosing the right care option for our child is not just about ensuring our child does not have negative experiences, it is also about making sure that our child's emotional and psychological development is nurtured and enhanced. This involves three things:

- Choosing the right care options;
- Building a strong, constructive relationship with the carer;
- Being vigilant.

*Choosing the right care options:* When making decisions about what type of care will best promote our child's emotional well-being, one of the most important factors to consider is our child's age, maturity and personality.

From an emotional and developmental perspective, the younger our child is, the more important it is that he or she receives as much one-to-one care as possible during their waking hours. The older a child is the better able he or she is psychologically to cope with group-care. This is why traditionally children are not sent to school before the age of four or five. A child will do best in group-care if they can walk, play with other children, share, feed themselves and speak. This is not to say that a young baby who hasn't yet developed these skills will be emotionally damaged by group-care, but their emotional well-being will require intensive individual input and attention within a group-care setting.

Other factors to consider are our child's personality and position within the family. A quiet, insecure child might benefit from one-to-one care, while a lively, outgoing child might do better in group-care or vice versa depending on the care. An only child might benefit from a group-care situation where there is an opportunity to interact with other children, while a middle child from a large family might benefit from a one-to-one care situation, receiving more personal attention.

The second most important factor to consider is the quality of care being provided. It is important to assess why a person is interested in providing care to our child. We need to be sure that a large part of the person's motivation is an interest and commitment to our child, or children in general, and a desire to look after and nurture children. While the person we select to care for our child does not have to have a professional qualification, it is important to know what experience the person has in caring for children. With family members, this is usually easy to assess, but with some child-minders, assessing this can be difficult. It is important to ask carers what their experience is and to seek information from others who know them or have used their services in the past. The physical environment in which our child is being cared for is also an important contributor to their emotional health.

It is important, in group-care situations such as crèches and nurseries, that some, if not all staff have recognised professional qualifications, and that the staff have the qualifications necessary to do the job they are being asked to do. It is also important to ensure that there are practice guidelines and child protection guidelines existing within the facility and that these are made available to parents. When we are choosing formal child-care options it is important to ensure that the person we choose to care for our child and anybody else working or living in the caring facility have been vetted. The crèche, playschool or nursery should also be registered with the appropriate statutory authorities.

*Building a strong, constructive relationship with the carer:* If our child is to thrive emotionally he or she needs to receive consistent parenting, both from the carer and from us. In implementing the approaches outlined in chapters two and three we need to ensure as best we can that the carer is doing likewise. In particular, we should try to agree with the carer the important components of parenting: how we discipline our child; how we support and reward our child; and how we communicate with our child. To achieve this, consistent regular communication with the carer is crucial. If our child's carer is good, we will learn something from them and they will learn from us. It is important that there is mutual respect between us. This will build our child's emotional security and sense of self-worth.

*Being vigilant:* How well our child's emotional well-being is being nurtured and enhanced by our carer will be reflected in their developmental progress, the quality of interaction between them and the carer, the quality of interaction between the carer and parents in general and the quality of interaction between the carers themselves. To ensure the caring environment remains emotionally healthy we need to monitor and be vigilant to these factors. This is best done by listening to and observing how our child is doing, which will be evident through their behaviour and language. Equally we will be able to do this by listening to and observing what the carer is saying and doing. Most importantly we need to trust our instincts. We will pick up on clues and act accordingly if things are not right.

**EXERCISE:** CREATING AN EMOTIONALLY HEALTHY CHILD-CARE ENVIRONMENT

Take no more than three minutes to complete each of these questions as honestly as you can. Move on to the next question after three minutes and leave any you can't complete unanswered. Do the exercise for each of your children separately.

| 98 | What does your child like most about the carer? |
|----|------------------------------------------------|
| 99 | What does the carer like most about him/her? |
| 100 | What is the carer's biggest strength? |
| 101 | What is the nicest thing the carer has said about your child? |
| 102 | What is the nicest thing your child has said or shown about the carer? |
| 103 | What makes you feel most secure about the carer? |

This exercise is designed to help us reflect on the strengths and emotional health of the child-care arrangements we have established for our child. The exercise seeks to remind and reinforce for us the reasons we chose this particular care arrangement. Our answers can give us security and confidence that our child is benefiting emotionally from this one.

Considering the questions we found difficult or could not answer is important. If we feel we have not given the answers enough thought it is worthwhile to give them further attention. If we feel our difficulties are related to the type of care our child is receiving or our inability to identify the strengths of this care it is important that we take the appropriate actions to address this. The care our child receives will play an important part in their emotional development and welfare.

Those who look after our children for short periods while we are socialising can also play an important role in enhancing our child's emotional well-being. It is important to apply the same principles to our babysitting arrangements as we would to formal child-care arrangements.

## Creating an emotionally healthy school environment

Our children spend approximately one-third of their childhoods in school. Their experiences here impact immensely on their emotional well-being and development. In particular this experience has a major bearing on how they view themselves socially and intellectually, and whether they believe they are clever, good at achieving things and popular. Their experiences in school teach them how to get on with others, how to work and how to compete. For this reason, it is very important that the school to which we send our child provides the best opportunity for them to protect and enhance their emotional health. Academic achievement is secondary to this key priority and indeed without emotional health academic achievement becomes irrelevant.

Of course, parents cannot control or plan for everything that happens in school but they can take some important steps to safeguard their child's school experiences. The most important of these are:

- Choosing schools wisely;
- Building appropriate and constructive relationships with the school staff;
- Being vigilant.

*Choosing schools wisely*: Picking a school that will best enhance our child's emotional welfare involves trying to match our child's personality with the characteristics of the school. Different schools suit different children. Some children do very well in academically-focused schools while others do better in a vocational environment. Some will respond well to strict discipline while others will prefer a less controlled regime. Some find it difficult to make new friends while others find it easy.

Most parents will have a good idea of the type of school environment that will best suit their child, and of course as our child gets older they will be able to tell us what type of school they feel suits them. The most important characteristic to consider is the school's educational ethos. Our child will benefit most if they receive a rounded education that includes academic, social and physical education. Most importantly, a good educational ethos will help a child achieve their individual potential in these three areas, enhancing their sense of self-worth and self-esteem and enhancing their opinion of themselves as achievers. Consideration of the physical environment should include how our child gets to school to ensure this does not add emotional stress to their lives. For instance, are they old enough to take the school bus? Is it supervised? Do they have to walk long distances? Sometimes, because of where we live, there may not be a choice of what school to send our child to. This makes being involved and influencing the school ethos even more important.

*Building appropriate and constructive relationships with the school staff* and *being vigilant* are essential. Once our child has started in a school it is important that we trust in our decision and invest everything we can into their school experience. It is important we do this in a balanced, constructive way. Appropriate involvement is important but over or under involvement should be avoided.

**HELP SHEET: Building good relationships with school staff and being vigilant**

| | Listening and communicating with our child about school | Teaching personal and emotional safety skills | Working in partnership with the school | Resolving our own school experiences | Knowing our child's school friends |
|---|---|---|---|---|---|
| **5–12 YEARS** | Ask about what happened in school each day in a way our child can answer. Did you do art today? Did you enjoy it? Reinforce the good things and monitor the negative things. Encourage positive participation and involvement. If they stop talking about school find out why. Take upset or unhappiness about school seriously. | Talk about what our child can do if he/she becomes upset in school. Talk about how to avoid negative situations in school. Talk about what our child can do if they become tired in school or don't want to do something. | Attend meetings, particularly with the teacher. Get involved in opportunities to participate. Bring problems to the attention of the school quickly and constructively. Focus on the positive aspects of the school. | Be aware of our own school experiences and do not let them influence our views of our child's school experiences. Take our lead from our child. Don't try to relive our school experiences through our child. | Invite school friends to the house. Listen when our child is discussing friends. Act constructively if difficulties arise with friends. Encourage our child to bring friends over. Take note if there is an unexplained sudden change of friends. |
| **13–19 YEARS** | Listen when they decide to talk about school – heed what is being said. | Discuss emotions and feelings with our child when they decide to discuss them. Focus on positive feelings generated by school. Discuss constructive ways to resolve school-related emotional problems. | Attend meetings and events. Take the lead from our child and get as involved as our child wishes us to be. Address difficulties constructively. | Be aware of our own school experiences and do not let them influence our views of our child's school experiences. Take our lead from our child. Don't try to relive our school experiences through our child. | Take note if patterns of socialising with friends change. Support our child to resolve difficulties with friends. Act constructively if our child cannot resolve difficulties. |

**EXERCISE: CREATING AN EMOTIONALLY HEALTHY SCHOOL ENVIRONMENT**

Take no more than three minutes to complete each of these questions as honestly as you can. Move on to the next question after three minutes and leave any you can't complete unanswered. Do the exercise for each of your children separately.

| 104 | What was it about your child's school that originally attracted you? |
|-----|---------------------------------------------------------------------|
| 105 | What is the best thing about your child's school? |
| 106 | What positive thing did your child say about the school this week? |
| 107 | What does your child do well at in school? |
| 108 | What was the most recent event you attended or participated in at the school? |
| 109 | What is the best thing about your child's school friends? |

This exercise is designed to help us reflect on our child's school experience and how this enhances their emotional well-being. It prompts us to recall the reasons we made the decisions to choose the school in the first place and what aspects of the school we feel are positive. Our answers help us to appreciate how school experiences are benefitting our child and can give us impetus to develop these particular strengths. Considering the questions we found difficult or could not answer is also useful. These may indicate that we have taken our attention off our child's schooling and that it might be useful to re-engage or refocus ourselves on this aspect of our child's life. It might suggest that at present our child's school experience is not positive and that this needs to be addressed.

## Bullying

Although bullying can occur in any setting, it is probably one of the biggest risks to our child's emotional health in school. Bullying is described as continuous physical, verbal or psychological intimidation of a child and by its very definition has a negative impact on a child's emotional well-being. While bullying has always been a feature of childhood, the internet and mobile phones have added a new dimension. It is likely that most children will experience bullying at some stage in their childhoods and some will experience it at a severe level. Talking and listening to our children about bullying, monitoring it if problems start to arise and supporting them to address bullying if it occurs are essential. When deciding whether to intervene or how to intervene the first consideration should be our child's emotional well-being.

## Private tuition/grinds

Many children now receive private or additional tuition as part of their education. It is important that we apply the same degree of caution in choosing a tutor as we do in choosing a school. We also need to be careful that we do not rely too much on private tuition or pressurise our child through its use. Given the length and intensity of the school day, private tuition should only be used when absolutely necessary and in full agreement with our child. The key principle guiding this decision should be our child's emotional well-being.

## Creating an emotionally healthy social environment for our child

For children to have balanced lives and to develop healthily, it is important that they get the opportunity to engage in social, leisure and sporting activities. While younger children are usually accompanied by their parents to such activities, as they grow older they engage more and more in activities that we are not directly supervising. Children benefit from social and leisure time with their parents but also need and benefit from such time with others. Parents cannot control all their child's experiences in these situations but as with school, if we chose their activities wisely, build good relationships with those running the activities and stay vigilant, we can ensure these activities are emotionally enhancing.

## HELP SHEET: Creating an Emotionally Healthy Social Environment

| |
|---|
| The organisation running the activities welcomes questions about their activities and the safety of their environment. |
| The organisation has a child protection policy and a proper recruitment process. |
| Staff and or volunteers seem competent and qualified for the activity they are running, are positive and enthusiastic in their approach to children and are able to maintain, control and discipline in a constructive and encouraging manner. |
| The importance of fun and fair play is encouraged. |
| The participation of parents is encouraged as much as possible. |
| Someone is in charge that supervises staff and volunteers. |
| The organisation meets appropriate health and safety regulations. |
| The self-esteem of children and young people is promoted and bullying and other aggressive behaviours are discouraged. |
| Activities are suitable for the age, experience and ability of the participants. |
| Children are adequately prepared for the activity being undertaken. |
| Travel is adequately supervised and organised. |
| The use of drugs, alcohol and tobacco is prohibited. |
| The staff and volunteers running activities respect the rights, dignity and worth of every child and treat everyone equally. |
| All children are given sufficient opportunity to participate in the activity and are made to feel and believe that they all have an equally important contribution to make to the activity. |
| Enjoying the activity is emphasised rather than just winning or being the best. |
| Sanctions are used in a corrective way and any interpreted as being humiliating or improper are not used. |
| The activity is held in an appropriate venue. |
| We can communicate our expectations to those running the activity, giving them the opportunity to tell us if they are not in a position to meet these expectations. |
| We have an agreement with the people running the activity about how we expect our child to participate and to be cared for. |
| We can stay and watch the activities and support our child when appropriate. |
| We feel we can offer support to the staff and volunteers or can take an active role in the organisation. |
| We listen to what our child is saying about the activities and seek constant feedback. |
| We are aware of and have resolved our own attitudes to sport and leisure activities: what's the point unless you are winning or the best; I wasn't good at this so neither will my child; it's just silly and won't help my child get on in life. |

**EXERCISE: CREATING AN EMOTIONALLY HEALTHY SOCIAL ENVIRONMENT**

Take no more than three minutes to complete each of these questions as honestly as you can. Move on to the next question after three minutes and leave any you can't complete unanswered. Do the exercise for each of your children separately.

| 110 | What social, sport or leisure activity does your child really like? |
|-----|---|
| 111 | How does he/she say this activity makes them feel? |
| 112 | What is the particular strength of the person who runs the activity? |
| 113 | What did you do recently to support your child's involvement in the activity? |
| 114 | When is the last time you talked to your child about the activity? |
| 115 | When you were a child what social, sport, leisure or social activity did you like to do? |

This exercise focuses on our child's social environment and the benefits of this environment on their emotional development. Our answers help us to appreciate the importance of social outlets for our child but also give us momentum to build on and develop the particular strengths of these experiences.

The questions we found difficult to answer or could not answer help us to assess whether our child is obtaining positive experiences from their social environment or whether we are giving this area of our child's life enough attention at the moment. These questions might serve as an incentive for us to focus more on our child's social outlets and on ensuring they are made more positive.

The last question in this exercise is designed to help us reflect on the social environment we experienced as children. It helps us to acknowledge the legacies from our own childhood and how this might be impacting on the decisions we make regarding our child's social environment.

## Holidays

While on holiday it is important that we apply the same principles to the activities our child is engaging in, particularly if we are not directly involved with these activities ourselves. Similarly, decisions to allow our child to go away on holiday with friends or relatives or even to go on sleepovers need to be taken on the basis of the likely impact on their emotional well-being and on the basis of the principles we have discussed. Our child will know themselves when they are emotionally ready to engage in these activities without us; being sensitive to what they are telling us is important. Sometimes a child might feel pressurised to agree to go because others are going and we need to support them to make their own decisions. Likewise, we need to place our knowledge of our child and their safety at the forefront of our considerations when deciding whether to allow them to engage in these types of activities no matter what other parents are doing. Sometimes, depending on the age of our child, we may have to overrule our child's stated wishes if we feel we cannot ensure their emotional or physical safety. There will always be other holidays or other sleepovers. Any activity will impact on our child's emotional welfare and we need to do the best we can to ensure the impact is positive.

## Creating emotionally healthy friendships

Friends are particularly important to our child's emotional development and our child plays a key role in their friend's emotional development. Indeed, friends are important throughout a person's life.

As children progress through childhood their friends become more important to them as their parents become a little less. The importance of friends only starts to diminish when a person becomes a parent themselves. When our children become adults, friends once again become more important in our lives.

Emotional connectedness is probably the central factor that determines who we choose as our friends. While the friendship process continues throughout our lives an understanding of how to make and keep friends occurs in childhood. Although our child will ultimately choose their own friends, parents have an important role to play in ensuring, as best we can, that their friendships are emotionally healthy.

The younger our child is the easier it is for us to influence who they choose as friends. The friendship process usually begins with us inviting other children to play and spend time with our child and vice versa. Even at this young age our child will begin to choose who they themselves want as their friends. Our main role is therefore to guide and support our child through the friendship process by accepting those they chose as their friends, teaching them how friends treat each other, helping them resolve difficulties and being a support to them when relationships break down.

The key principle underpinning all of these roles should be the enhancement of our child's emotional well-being. This may require us to directly intervene in our child's friendships at times, but such involvement needs to be handled sensitively and again with the primary purpose of enhancing our child's emotional well-being. The older our child is, the more reluctant we should be to intervene directly and our role at this stage needs to focus on supporting him/ her to do what they think they need to do.

**Creating an emotionally healthy internet environment**

Our children have been born into an internet age and the internet is now an integral part of all of our lives. Over the last ten years, we have seen one of the greatest transformations in the way that we communicate with each other, get our information, tell others about ourselves and do business. While for parents this has been a transformation, for our children it is simply their world.

Almost all children aged ten and older have access to the internet through mobile phones or computers. The advances in communications systems present great opportunities for children but also carry some risks, particularly to their emotional well-being.

For children, the internet provides a rich source of information and communication. It opens up the opportunity for them to expand their thinking and outlook on life and to communicate with people who have the same interests as they have. For socially-isolated children, it provides an opportunity to communicate with others in a less threatening way, and for some, it provides the opportunity to access information from a variety of different perspectives and to learn about different possible life choices. It opens up an unlimited vista of opportunity and ideas for children. In this regard the internet, when used properly, enhances and enriches our child's emotional well-being.

Because of the unlimited potential of the internet, children need parental input and guidance to ensure that their usage and involvement is safe and beneficial. The difficulty is that many parents have limited knowledge of the internet and how it works. Often children are more comfortable than we are around mobile phones and computers. Because of its power, reach, lack of limits and attraction, the internet also carries additional risks to emotional well-being such as access to inappropriate, violent or sexual material, the potential to make contact with dangerous people who may exploit their vulnerabilities, or the risk of having their personal details exploited.

These dangers, while important to consider, need to be kept in perspective. With the right approach and input the internet can benefit our child's emotional well-being.

**HELP SHEET: Creating an Emotionally Healthy Internet Environment**

| | **Building our own knowledge** Learning about and having a reasonable understanding of how the internet works is now essential to parenting. | **Integrating technology into parenting** The best way to ensure children benefit emotionally from the internet is to ensure it becomes a normal, everyday part of our parenting and relationship with our child. | **Establishing the rules** Like any other activity our child engages in, we need to agree the rules of usage. | **Discussing the advantages and the risks** Maintaining the internet as a positive influence in our child's life involves ensuring they know about the positives and the negatives of its usage. | **Trusting our child and giving them responsibility** As with all other activities our child engages in, the best approach is to invest trust in our child at an appropriate level for their age and maturity. |
|---|---|---|---|---|---|
| **0–8 YEARS** | If we haven't done so before we should start to explore the simple things about the internet and how it works, such as sending emails, how to access sites, so that we are prepared when our child starts to want to learn about the internet.<br>We need to start learning the principles of services such as Facebook, WhatsApp, etc. and how iCloud works when our child is this age so we are prepared for when they are older and can know as much as they will learn quickly<br>Modelling disciplined usage. | Exploring the internet with our child. Finding age-appropriate games and teaching our child how to use a tablet or computer. | Ensuring they cannot access the internet accidently without us. | Showing them how good the internet can be and the good material available. | Reinforcing how good they are at using a tablet or computer and at finding their way around the internet. |

| | | | | | |
|---|---|---|---|---|---|
| **8–12 YEARS** | We need to start learning the principles of Facebook, WhatsApp and how the iCloud works when our child is this age so we are prepared to answer their questions when they are older.<br><br>Modelling disciplined usage. | Encouraging them to use the internet to contact and communicate with you and their friends in a balanced way. | Ensuring that they can only access the internet with us or with our permission.<br><br>Ensuring unsuitable sites are blocked.<br><br>Agreeing that they will tell us if they accidentally come across anything upsetting to them. | Showing them how good the internet can be and the good material available.<br><br>Raising their awareness of the risks without being too explicit. 'Sometimes there are things on the internet that might upset us so we don't want to see that, sometimes there are things that are private to us that we don't want other people knowing, sometimes strangers can try to contact you on the internet and if that happens it's important you tell me.' | Acknowledging when they have used the internet to find out something or contact somebody successfully.<br><br>Reinforcing how clever they are with the internet.<br><br>Giving them positive feedback for bringing problems to our attention. |
| **12–17 YEARS** | Engaging in appropriate social networking sites and exploring the advantages and dangers.<br><br>Learning about the main apps our child is using and understanding the advantages and dangers.<br><br>Modelling disciplined usage. | Encouraging them to use the internet to contact and communicate with you and their friends in a balanced way.<br><br>Encouraging them to engage in appropriate social networking sites with us supervising and guiding the information they give and the interactions they have in the beginning. | Ensuring unsuitable sites are blocked.<br><br>Agreeing that they will tell us if they come across anything upsetting on the internet.<br><br>Agreeing that they will be careful about the things they share about themselves on the internet and if they are unsure they will discuss them with us.<br><br>Agreeing the amount of time they will use the internet for social purposes. | Discussing the latest apps and internet advantages and how it can help with projects, homework and keeping in touch with friends.<br><br>Being explicit about the risks. 'There is some material that is not nice and not accurate on the internet about sex and violence, which we don't want to see. Sharing too much of our personal information could be used by others to hurt us. People who might want to harm us could try to contact us on the internet.' | Allowing them to engage in the internet without our supervision.<br><br>Reinforcing from time to time how we trust them on the internet and how we know they will bring any difficulties to our attention.<br><br>Respecting their privacy unless serious problems arise. |

| **18–21 YEARS** | | | | |
|---|---|---|---|---|
| Engaging in appropriate social networking sites and exploring the advantages and dangers. Learning about the main apps young adults are using and understanding the advantages and dangers. Modelling disciplined usage. | Communicating with them through the internet when appropriate. | Encouraging them to tell us if they come across anything upsetting on the internet. Agreeing that they will be careful about the things they share about themselves online. | Discussing the advantages and disadvantages openly. 'Isn't it great how easy it is to contact people using Facebook; it's terrible the amount of pornography that you can easily come across on the internet; its sad the way some people put up photos of themselves that they will regret later.' | Respecting their privacy. |

**EXERCISE: CREATING AN EMOTIONALLY HEALTHY INTERNET ENVIRONMENT**

Take no more than three minutes to complete each of these questions as honestly as you can. Move on to the next question after three minutes and leave any you can't complete unanswered. Do the exercise for each of your children separately.

| 116 | What do you enjoy doing with your child on the internet? |
|---|---|
| 117 | What does your child most enjoy doing on the internet? |
| 118 | What is the latest thing you taught your child about the internet? |
| 119 | What is the latest thing your child has taught you about the internet? |
| 120 | What is the most important rule you have about the internet? |
| 121 | What is the latest thing you have discussed with your child about the internet? |

This exercise is designed to help us reflect on the positive aspects of the internet and how it can be utilised as an opportunity for us to spend quality time with our child. The answers to these questions help us to appreciate the benefits of the internet and how it can be utilised both by ourselves and our child to enhance their emotional well-being and development.

Considering the questions we found difficult to answer or could not answer is also beneficial. These might suggest that we have not given this aspect of our child's experiences enough consideration or that we believe our child's and our own involvement with the internet is predominantly negative. The internet is now an integral part of all of our lives and so ensuring that we reflect on our child's experiences of this is important to their emotional development. If this exercise raises concerns this should be used as an opportunity to address things we are not happy with regarding our child's use or experience of the internet.

## Compulsive usage

Because of its attraction, particularly to children, the internet can be easily overused and for some children can become compulsive and addictive. Research findings on the impact of the use of the internet are somewhat contradictory. Some of the earliest studies, such as one carried out by researchers at Carnegie-Mellon University in the USA in 1998, found evidence they called the internet paradox: greater internet usage is associated with decreased psychological well-being and social involvement (Kraut 1998). Since this study there have been others that have negated these findings (Jackson 2004).

However we know that children who spend too much time on the internet miss out on those extremely important social and emotional experiences that can only be obtained through face-to-face contact with others. Physical activity, peer interaction, imaginative and exploratory play are also all impacted upon. In addition, there is a risk that children exposed to a virtual world can begin to become detached from reality, with their involvement in everyday activities becoming even more limited. Parents need to try, as best they can, to ensure their child spends an appropriate amount of time on the internet and balances this with other activities. The daily activity chart is a useful way to gauge this.

## Instructions

Fill in the daily activity chart below based on your child's average week. Mark each hour according to the main activity your child is involved in during that hour.

\# For time spent on a hobby or relaxing

‖ For time spent at school and on schoolwork

• For time spent engaging in sport, social or leisure activities

× For time spent with you directly

≠ For time spent on the internet

| | Mon | Tue | Wed | Thu | Fri | Sat | Sun |
|---|---|---|---|---|---|---|---|
| 08.00 – 09.00 | | | | | | | |
| 09.00 – 10.00 | | | | | | | |
| 10.00 – 11.00 | | | | | | | |
| 11.00 – 12.00 | | | | | | | |
| 12.00 – 13.00 | | | | | | | |
| 13.00 – 14.00 | | | | | | | |
| 14.00 – 15.00 | | | | | | | |
| 15.00 – 16.00 | | | | | | | |
| 16.00 – 17.00 | | | | | | | |
| 17.00 – 18.00 | | | | | | | |
| 18.00 – 19.00 | | | | | | | |
| 19.00 – 20.00 | | | | | | | |
| 20.00 – 21.00 | | | | | | | |
| 21.00 – 22.00 | | | | | | | |
| 22.00 – 23.00 | | | | | | | |
| 23.00 – 24.00 | | | | | | | |

When you have completed the chart, add up the symbols and fill in the graph on the next page. Reflect on the final graph and consider whether you feel it represents a balanced lifestyle for your child.

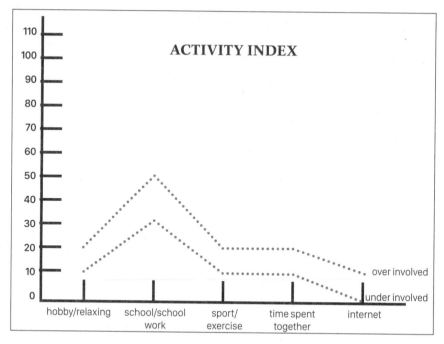

This chart can also be applied to assess your child's involvement in other social activities.

Modelling good behaviour in regards to internet usage is important. How we ourselves interact and use the internet should reflect the principles discussed above. Applying the above exercise to our own internet usage can also be insightful.

## Risks to emotional health

While there are a number of environmental experiences that can negatively impact on our child's emotional health, two warrant specific mention: drug and alcohol abuse; and premature sexualisation.

It is an unfortunate reality that for our children drugs and alcohol are freely available in most communities. The 2006 Irish government study, State of the Nation's Children, reported that fifty-seven per cent of fifteen-year-olds admitted to binge drinking while the European School Survey Project on Alcohol and Other Drugs (2003) found that forty per cent of Irish children aged fifteen reported using an illicit drug. Aside from the physical risks, the emotional and psychological consequences of drug and alcohol misuse are immense, including poor school performance, social isolation, addiction and related mental health difficulties.

Within most modern societies, children are bombarded with a tremendous number of sexualised messages and images. The internet, digital television, magazines, advertisements and media reporting, all now portray sexualised images and messages. Pornography is freely accessible on the internet with over one-third of young people reporting visiting pornographic websites (Webwise 2006). Premature sexualisation of children impacts significantly on their emotional well-being. It deprives children of their right to have an innocent, carefree childhood and often forces them into communication and behaviour patterns that they do not fully understand. It also makes children more vulnerable to sexual exploitation.

### How do we best manage these risks?
Creating emotionally healthy environments helps protect our child from these experiences. Building our child's emotional health and psychological resilience also helps protect them against being adversely affected by emotionally unhealthy experiences. However, no matter how emotionally healthy or psychologically healthy our child is they will not be able to manage sustained exposure to such experiences. In dealing with drug and alcohol use and premature sexualisation there are a number of additional measures that we should try to take.

*Communicating about alcohol, drugs and sexuality:* Communicating with our child about these issues helps them deal with them when they arise. Listening carefully to what our child is telling us about how he/she is learning, seeing and experiencing these issues is important. Talking with our child about the attractions and dangers of engaging in drug and alcohol usage and sexual behaviour helps them make the right choices and options. These discussions need to commence before the teenage years and need to be grounded in trust, honesty and tolerance.

To help our child make the right decisions it is important that we give him or her as much accurate and appropriate information as we can. We need to take a lifelong learning approach to educating our child on these issues, starting as early as possible and continuing throughout childhood and adolescence.

The amount and type of information we give our child and the way we present it to them should be determined by their age and maturity.

While we should only ever give our child the information he or she is capable of handling, we should be careful not to limit the information because of our own prejudices or discomfort. Exploring what our child knows already with open-ended questions, being guided by the questions our child asks us and regularly checking with them if they want us to give them more information are all useful ways to get the balance right.

*Monitoring our child's behaviour*: Getting the balance between appropriately monitoring our child's behaviour and not smothering them is one of the hardest things for a parent to get right. When it comes to alcohol, drugs and sexuality this balance is extremely important. For example, it is likely that children who are over-controlled or under-controlled by parents are more likely to misuse drugs. The best and most effective way of monitoring our children is to invest in our relationship with them as long as we feel it is prudent to do so. Most children welcome the security of knowing that their parents care enough about them to check on them and set limits.

*Modelling good behaviour:* Living our beliefs and values helps our child to make the right choices. Modelling good behaviour regarding drugs, alcohol, sex and self-worth is one of the most effective ways we can protect our child from these risks. While our children will have their own individual ways of dealing with these challenges, it is useful for us to draw from our own experiences of how we dealt with them when we were children.

*Supporting our child when difficulties arise:* Difficulties involving drugs, alcohol or sexual behaviour often spark strong emotions in parents, sometimes making it difficult for us to be supportive. It is usual to feel we have let our child down or he/she has let us down. Sometimes we feel powerless. What is important to remember is that we know our child best and we are the people best placed to support and help them. It is important when confronted with such difficulties that we are able to set aside or control our own emotions and focus ourselves on supporting our child. This often involves us challenging some of our own experiences and beliefs about alcohol, drug use and sexuality. We may have used or still use alcohol and drugs or may have engaged in sexual behaviour as a child or adolescent. We may feel these are all normal childhood experiences. Resolving these experiences and beliefs is essential if we are to support our child.

Our aim as parents should be to prevent our child ever using drugs or engaging in sexual activity before they are ready to do so. The older a person is when he or she first takes an alcoholic drink or first engages in sexual activity, the more likely he/she will be able to make an informed decision about this activity and to understand and deal with the emotional consequences of their actions. For this reason, we should try to ensure our child first tries or experiences these activities when they are mature enough to do so.

| EXERCISE: DEALING WITH, ALCOHOL, DRUGS AND EARLY SEXUALISATION |
|---|
| Take no more than three minutes to complete each of these questions as honestly as you can. Move on to the next question after three minutes and leave any you can't complete unanswered. Do the exercise for each of your children separately. |

| | |
|---|---|
| 122 | What is the most recent thing you have discussed with your child about alcohol? |
| 123 | What is the most recent thing you have discussed with your child about drugs? |
| 124 | What is the latest issue you have discussed with your child about sex? |
| 125 | What age were you when you tried your first alcoholic drink and how did it feel? |
| 126 | What age were you when you tried your first drug and how did it feel? |
| 127 | What age were you when you first engaged in sexual activity and how did it feel? |

This exercise is designed to help us reflect on the issues of alcohol, drugs and sexual activity and how we can best prepare our child for their engagement with these aspects of life. Our answers to these questions will help us to consider whether we are actively discussing these topics with our child and preparing them for how they might manage their interactions with them in the future. The exercise also helps us to recall how we dealt with and engaged with alcohol, drugs and sexual activity when we were children and teenagers. The importance of these questions is to help us to assess whether our engagement is having any impact on how we are preparing our child for their engagement.

Reflecting on questions we found difficult or could not answer is also important. These could suggest that we have not given this area of parenting much consideration as yet or that we find this particular area difficult to address with our child. Unanswered questions provide us with an opportunity to commence the discussion process, which is important in terms of helping our child deal with the emotional aspects of alcohol, drugs and sexualisation.

## Keeping risks in perspective

Although we always want to do our best for our child it is also important that we keep risks in perspective. Being overly cautious or overly involved can smother our child and this can have an adverse impact on their emotional health. One useful tool for creating emotionally healthy environments while keeping risks in perspective is to set up our own Child Risk Assessment system. While this might seem like a very structured or formal way to review our child's environment and activities it can help put our minds at rest about the things we are worried about and give us more security. It is useful to do this exercise at different times in our child's life, particularly if we begin to get worried about a new development or if we are confronted with a worrying decision.

## Child Risk Assessment

The Child Risk Assessment is a structured method for parents to assess psychological and emotional risks their child might face, how serious these risks are and how best to address them. It can also be used to assess physical risks. The Child Risk Assessment involves the following steps:

1. Write down all the issues that you are worried about regarding your child. Be as honest as you can: 'my child might not make friends in school.'

2. Write down the main emotional or psychological effects that could occur as a result of this risk (the implications): 'she will become lonely and depressed'; 'she will become socially isolated'; 'she will start missing school'.

3. Rate how important this issue is to your child on a scale of one to five: one being not at all important and five being very important. For example: 'making friends at school is very important to my child so I will give this a five.'

4. Rate how likely this issue is to arise on a scale of one to five, one being not likely and five being very likely: 'My child is quiet, she finds it hard to mix in groups, she worries a lot in social situations. However she has a small number of very good friends who live nearby. On balance it is quite likely that she will have some difficulty making friends in school so I will give this a four.'

5. Calculate a risk score by multiplying the two scores together. An issue receiving a score of over twenty is one you need to take actions to address; one that receives between fifteen and twenty is worth monitoring; while anything rated lower can be dismissed. 'This risk is rated as a four by five equalling twenty and therefore needs to be addressed.'

6. Write down what you can do to address the risks you have identified as serious and keep this for the future. For example: 'I am going to encourage my child to invite her class mates over after school once a week, make sure she stays friendly with and sees her local friends regularly and monitor, in a subtle way, who she is spending her lunchtimes with.'

The chart below provides a useful means for conducting this assessment, although a blank piece of paper works equally as well. The important thing to remember is to have faith in your own judgement. All children are subject to dangers and risks. We cannot cripple them or ourselves by overly exaggerating these risks, but equally it is important that we identify the ones that are most serious and try to address these as best we can. Some risks we can do nothing about and part of this exercise is to identify these and then forget about them. As our child grows older and begins to do new things it is always useful to repeat the exercise to ensure we keep on top of risks and keep them in perspective.

| Ref | Risk | Implications | Significance (A) | Likelihood (B) | Risk Score (C) | Actions to take |
|---|---|---|---|---|---|---|
| Example | My child might not make friends in school. | She will become lonely. She might become depressed. She might become socially isolated. | 5 | 4 | 20 | Invite school class mates over to the house once a week. Strengthen relationships with existing friends. Keep the situation monitored. |
| 1 | | | | | | |
| 2 | | | | | | |
| 3 | | | | | | |
| 4 | | | | | | |
| 5 | | | | | | |

Sometimes it is useful to list the top risks and then check them a month or two later to see if the actions you have taken have changed things. If not you can come up with some new actions, but if it has changed then it is time to forget about this issue. For instance, my child has started to pal around with two girls from school and one invites her to her house regularly so I am going to forget this issue for now.

| TOP RISKS | | | | |
|---|---|---|---|---|
| Ref | Risk | Risk score 3 months ago | Risk score now | Change & purposed actions |
| Example | Not making friends at school | 20 | (5 sig x 2 likl)=10 | Forget |
| 1 | | | | |
| 2 | | | | |
| 3 | | | | |
| 4 | | | | |
| 5 | | | | |
| 6 | | | | |
| 7 | | | | |
| 8 | | | | |

## Summary

The job of parenting is demanding and busy enough without trying to monitor every experience our child has. As we discussed in chapters two and three our child's emotional health and psychological resilience will be best enhanced by our direct engagement with them, teaching them how to be happy and how to feel good about themselves. The most we can do after this is to try our best to ensure our child's experiences, on balance, enhance their emotional well-being rather than weaken or damage it. Trying to do any more will smother our child and cause us stress and dissatisfaction.

# six

## *Loving Ourselves*

'And then one day you realise that your children are worrying about you. You wonder how you let your guard down and then it dawns on you that your well-being is their well-being, that they love you as much as you love them.'

To be able to look after our child's emotional health, we need to be able to look after our own emotional health. For these reasons we need to do everything we can to keep ourselves emotionally healthy. As with children, protecting our own emotional health requires four skills:

- Connecting with our inner parent;
- Knowing how to be happy, particularly happy parents;
- Believing that we are good people and particularly good parents;
- Ensuring that the environment in which we live and parent is emotionally healthy.

Having good emotional health and strong psychological resilience not only helps us enjoy the good aspects of parenting but also helps us get through the difficult times. Poor emotional health can make the challenges and setbacks which parenting inevitably brings harder to cope with.

A person's life satisfaction and happiness ratings can increase when they have children, which is also one of the factors that reduce our likelihood of developing mental health difficulties. But of course the benefits do not occur automatically. They require us to apply the core principles of good emotional health to our parenting.

## Connecting with our inner parent

As we discussed in chapter one, connecting with our inner parent is the essential first step in creating emotionally healthy children. It is also the first step in being an emotionally healthy parent. Believing that we have an innate love for our child and that we are prepared to do all we can to connect with and express this love helps us to feel at one with ourselves as a parent and as a person. Finding our true inner parent is a journey of discovery. Acknowledging and embarking on the journey places us on the road to emotional health.

When the journey towards connecting with our inner parent is delayed or blocked we experience emotional angst. Many factors can cause such blocks: unwanted pregnancy, relationship difficulties, over-involvement in career and pre-existing emotional difficulties among them. However, overcoming these is both essential and achievable. No matter what our circumstances, at a psychological level, having a baby is always an active choice. No matter what emotional or relationship difficulties we face, with the right insight and support these do not have to interfere with us connecting with our love for our child. If we open ourselves up to our child he/she will ensure we put our career in perspective. Connecting with our inner parent involves unearthing our innate love and re-energising ourselves by channelling this emotion.

## Knowing how to be happy and how to feel good about ourselves

People who are happy and who feel good about themselves will be emotionally healthy and psychologically resilient. They are likely to experience fewer emotional difficulties and when they do they are better able to deal with them and to recover. As we discussed in chapters two and three, both abilities are important in their own right but it is the combination of the two that creates sustainable and robust emotional health. These abilities, like all others, are learnt. As we progress through our lives and particularly through our parenting journey, these abilities, influenced by our experiences and mindset, will change.

Monitoring ourselves from time to time on these two parameters is a useful way of checking our emotional health. One tool for doing this is utilising the emotional health grid outlined in chapter two. Using the grid to assess our emotional health helps us to avoid or acknowledge when we are becoming emotionally insecure, emotionally dissatisfied or are beginning to have emotional difficulties, and to take actions to address this.

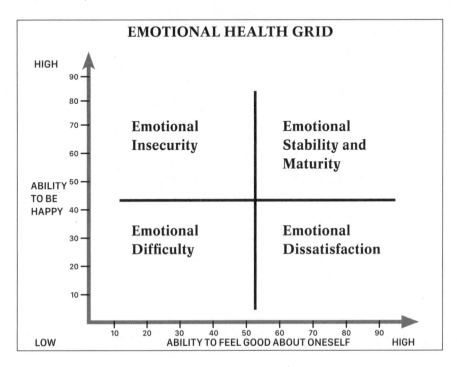

### Knowing how to be a happy parent

Having the ability to be happy is essential to being emotionally healthy. If, as children, we have learnt this ability, we are not only more likely to have had an emotionally healthy childhood but we also enhance the possibility of having an emotionally healthy adult life. However it is never too late to learn this ability and becoming a parent often gives us the necessary incentive.

Having the ability to be happy allows us to enjoy life. It increases the likelihood of us being healthy, expressive, creative and in touch with who we truly are. It does not mean that we will be happy all the time but it enables us to see the good that is in our lives and to enjoy life when it can be enjoyed. Developing this ability involves a number of simple but essential skills. Becoming a parent has the potential to increase our ability to be happy as a person if we get positive reinforcement from the parenting process.

Accepting that we are unique, with our own unique personality, helps us to see happiness in ourselves and enhances the vitality and richness of our lives. Nurturing our self-expression and personal characteristics and giving ourselves the freedom to 'be ourselves' is important to this process. Avoiding comparisons and conformity with others is essential.

Applying this individualism to our parenting gives us the best opportunity to realise our true potential as a parent. It also helps us to avoid the stress of trying to be a parent we are not. There is no perfect parent type. Our perfect parenting type is the one that fits best with our own and our child's individualism. Being ourselves as parents and freeing ourselves from the burden of comparisons and expectations makes us happier people and better parents. This also helps us to find our individualism as a person.

Looking for and seeing the best in ourselves and what we do is an important part of teaching ourselves how to be happy. Even when we make mistakes, or do things that we regret, realising that the totality of who we are is good and special is essential. This is particularly important when it comes to parenting. Seeing the best in our parenting selves makes it easier for us to recognise happiness, makes us better able to cope with criticism and negativity and enhances our emotional health.

| EXERCISE: PERSONAL PERCEPTION |
|---|
| Take no more than three minutes to complete each of these questions as honestly as you can. Move on to the next question after three minutes and leave any you can't complete unanswered. |

| 128 | What characteristics make you special? |
|---|---|
| 129 | What characteristics make you special as a parent? |
| 130 | What things do you do that make you different from other parents? |
| 131 | What are your strengths? |
| 132 | What are your strengths as a parent? |
| 133 | What are you proud of? |
| 134 | What are you proud of as a parent? |

This exercise is designed to help us reflect on what makes us special, both as an individual and as a parent and what we are particularly good at as a parent. It helps us to consider how good we are at looking at our strengths and our achievements as parents. The answers can both reinforce and reinvigorate us to continue on our journey of parenting discovery. Throughout the parenting journey it can be difficult not to get preoccupied with the difficulties and so our answers to this exercise help us to refocus on the positives.

Questions we find difficult or unable to answer may indicate that we have not given ourselves the opportunity to assess our parenting strengths and achievements. They may also indicate that we are preoccupied with our parenting challenges and with our weaknesses and have not been able to concentrate on the positives. From this perspective these questions provide us with the opportunity to refocus ourselves and commence the process of positive self-reinforcement.

## Knowing and understanding ourselves

Learning how to be happy requires us to understand ourselves and have an accurate and positive sense of ourselves. Emotional Intelligence – the ability to recognise, understand and deal with our own and other people's emotions – is an important part of knowing and understanding ourselves. If we have strong emotional intelligence, we will be better equipped to recognise happiness, sadness and stress. Recognising these emotions makes them easier to manage and respond to. Building self-awareness and emotional intelligence is a lifelong process and is different at different ages. The earlier we start the more at ease we will be as we progress through our lives. The stronger the foundations of self-awareness and emotional intelligence the harder it is to shake or unhinge them. However, it is never too late to start the process.

Becoming a parent often provides us with the impetus to look again at our self-awareness because it presents us with a new perspective of ourselves: being a parent. Building our child's self-awareness and emotional intelligence requires us as parents to have developed a strong sense of ourselves. The skills to do this are well worth considering in some detail:

- **Self-reflection:** Spending time reflecting on and thinking about our own actions, statements and feelings.

- **Talking:** Talking with those we trust about ourselves and our interactions with others.

- **Understanding and dealing with feelings:** Learning how to understand our feelings and to express them in appropriate, constructive ways.

- **Celebrating our strengths:** Developing insight and acknowledging what we are genuinely good at and being accepting of our weaknesses.

- **Nurturing our values:** Developing a sense of what we believe in and being comfortable with these beliefs.

**EXERCISE: SELF-AWARENESS AND EMOTIONAL INTELLIGENCE**

Take no more than three minutes to complete each of these questions as honestly as you can. Move on to the next question after three minutes and leave any you can't complete unanswered.

| | |
|---|---|
| 135 | What one thing about yourself do you reflect on most often? |
| 136 | What one thing that you did this week did you reflect on? |
| 137 | Who do you trust to talk to about yourself? |
| 138 | Who do you tell when you are feeling good about yourself? |
| 139 | How do people know when you are angry? |
| 140 | How do people know when you are happy? |
| 141 | Who do you trust enough to tell you are very good at something? |
| 142 | What are you very good at? |
| 143 | What value do you hold that you are prepared to tell people about? |
| 144 | Who do you talk to about your values? |
| 145 | What one value did you learn from your own parents? |

This exercise is designed to help us focus on our own self-awareness and emotional intelligence. It can be a challenging exercise because it is often difficult to reflect on how we interpret and deal with emotions and how we view ourselves. Our answers to these questions help us to gain some insight into how good we are at understanding ourselves and talking about our feelings and emotions. Two of the questions deal with the issue of values and again these answers help us to acknowledge what is important to us. Our answers provide us with an opportunity to remind ourselves of the importance of being able to consider and discuss our emotions and those aspects of ourselves that we feel are important.

Questions we found difficult or unable to answer can indicate a number of things. Sometimes we don't have the time or energy to concentrate on ourselves, our emotions or what is important to us, and therefore our unanswered questions may provide us with a reminder of how important this process is. These questions may also suggest to us that we have allowed ourselves to become a little isolated or reluctant to discuss some of our innermost feelings and values with others. The unanswered questions provide us with an opportunity to reassess these aspects of ourselves in the context of appreciating how important it is for us to build these skills in ourselves and in our child.

## Shaping our own thinking and behaviour

As we know, one of the most important determinants of how good we are at being happy is how we act, how these actions influence our thinking, and how we think about or interpret our life experiences. Positive behaviour not only helps us to be happy but also helps us develop a positive mindset. Similarly, having a positive mindset helps us to see the positive aspect of our actions. Our emotional mindset is ever evolving and is influenced by our personality and how we learn to emotionally interpret events and actions. While we all have positive and negative experiences in our lives, which we respond to in a positive or negative way, most everyday experiences are open to interpretation. Similarly, while we all have to engage in actions that make us feel bad from time to time mostly we have choices about what actions we take and what ones we don't. Shaping our thinking and behaviour involves distinct skills, the most important of which are the following:

- Actively practising the skills of positive action and thinking: making a conscious effort to smile, laugh, see the good in things; making positive statements, telling other people nice things, hearing nice things people say about us.

- Learning how to reframe: seeing the positives in what we do and how we handle situations, even difficult ones. Practising turning negative into positives. For instance, the boss gave out because I was late but that shows he depends on me; my child hates going to bed unless I read him a story but that shows that he loves his time with me.

- Learning and practising problem-solving skills: exploring possible solutions to problems and picking the best option.

- Rewarding ourselves for thinking and acting positively. For instance, I feel I responded well today when my son got really upset about his maths homework and started shouting at me. I stayed calm, reminded him that these exercises were particularly hard and that I wasn't even sure how to do them and agreed he should ask the teacher to show him how to do them again tomorrow. I also told him how good his English story was. I am going to relax now and watch my favourite TV show.

| EXERCISE: SHAPING THINKING AND BEHAVIOUR | |
|---|---|
| Take no more than three minutes to complete each of these questions as honestly as you can. Move on to the next question after three minutes and leave any you can't complete unanswered. | |
| 146 | What one very positive thought did you have this week? |
| 147 | What one very positive thing did you do this week? |
| 148 | What one potential negative action did you turn into a positive action this week? |
| 149 | What one negative thought did you turn into a positive thought this week? |
| 150 | What one good solution did you find to a problem this week? |

| 151 | What one solution did you find to a problem one of your children had this week? |
|---|---|
| 152 | What nice thing did you do for yourself this week? |
| 153 | What nice thing will you do for yourself next week? |

This exercise aims to help us consider how good we are at shaping our own thinking and behaviour. The focus of the exercise is on positive thinking and behaviour. Our answers help us to appreciate our skills in this area and can give us momentum to continue to develop and enhance these skills.

Unanswered or difficult to answer questions provide us with the opportunity to consider whether this is an area that needs some more attention. We may find it difficult to focus on the positive and to positively shape our thinking and our behaviour; if, on reflection, this emerges it is an opportunity for us to start to develop these particular skills.

Shaping our child's thinking and behaviour is made easier if we have developed the skills and insights to do this for ourselves.

Having the ability to be happy does not mean that we will be happy all of the time or will ignore sad or hurtful emotions. It does, however, arm us to see the good in life, to enjoy life when the opportunity arises, to better respond to the challenges of life and to be positive, constructive parents.

**Believing that we are good parents**
When we acknowledge and value ourselves as the very special person we are, our full intelligence, abilities and potential flourish. We all have our own innate wisdom, abilities, curiosity and sense of what is important to us, and when we accept and engage with these we enhance our emotional health and psychological resilience. Becoming a parent often provides us with the momentum to further learn and discover our true selves and to fulfil our true potential in our own unique way.

**Believing that we are loved and are lovable**
Believing that we are loved and are lovable is an essential part of the

journey towards believing we are good people. This is particularly important when we become a parent because we cannot connect with our inner love for our child unless we have connected with our love for ourselves. We are all loved by at least one person in our lives and drawing off this love makes us feel good about ourselves even in difficult times or when we have made mistakes. Feeling loved makes us emotionally stronger and frees us to love others. Reminding ourselves as often as we need to that we are loved protects us in times of difficulty. Of course our child will love us, and when we connect with this love it makes us emotionally stronger.

| EXERCISE: BEING LOVED |
|---|
| Take no more than three minutes to complete each of these questions as honestly as you can. Move on to the next question after three minutes and leave any you can't complete unanswered. |

| 154 | Who is one person who you know loves you? |
|---|---|
| 155 | How do you know they love you? |
| 156 | What is it about you that they love? |
| 157 | How does their love for you make you feel? |
| 158 | How do you know your child loves you? |
| 159 | How does your child's love for you make you feel? |
| 160 | What is it about you that is lovable? |

This exercise is focused on getting us to reflect on being loved. Two of the questions deal directly with being loved by our child. The exercise can be challenging because it asks us to consider aspects of ourselves that are deeply personal.

Our answers provide us with reinforcement and acknowledgement that we are not only lovable but that it is important to recognise this in ourselves. Reminding ourselves that we are loved by our child will enhance this special relationship.

Finding it difficult or being unable to answer these questions is worthy of consideration. Perhaps we haven't given this area of our lives much thought or, due to particular challenges or negative experiences, we are finding it difficult to focus on this aspect of our lives at the moment. Unanswered questions provide us with an opportunity to start or progress the journey towards understanding what makes us lovable and who loves us. Love is an essential part of raising emotionally healthy children and knowing that we are loved ourselves helps us to make our child feel loved.

## Spending time being good to ourselves

Feeling good about ourselves not only involves us thinking good things about ourselves but also involves us treating ourselves well. Staying physically well, getting enough sleep, giving ourselves space to relax, doing things we enjoy and spending time renewing our sense of self are all important. When we become a parent, being good to ourselves is essential. No matter how fulfilling we find parenting it still presents most of us with many lifestyle hurdles. In the early years getting enough sleep is one of the greatest hurdles and as our child or children grow up, simply finding time to exercise, relax, engage in hobbies and reflect is difficult. However we cannot support our child's emotional health if we do not feel good about ourselves. This requires us to be good to ourselves.

Each of us knows what achieves this best for us; it is finding the time which is the real skill. One useful way to monitor, assess and change how we manage this aspect of our lives is to use the daily activity chart on the next page for ourselves. Each day and each week will most likely be different and we cannot be all things to all people. However, from time to time it is useful to assess how balanced our lifestyle actually is and what changes we would like to make.

## Instructions

Fill in the daily activity chart below based on your average week. Mark each hour according to the main activity you are involved in during that hour.

\# For time spent parenting
‖ For time spent at work
• For time spent with your partner
× For time spent on hobbies, relaxing, reflecting
≠ For time spent exercising, sport

|  | Mon | Tue | Wed | Thu | Fri | Sat | Sun |
|---|---|---|---|---|---|---|---|
| 08.00 – 09.00 |  |  |  |  |  |  |  |
| 09.00 – 10.00 |  |  |  |  |  |  |  |
| 10.00 – 11.00 |  |  |  |  |  |  |  |
| 11.00 – 12.00 |  |  |  |  |  |  |  |
| 12.00 – 13.00 |  |  |  |  |  |  |  |
| 13.00 – 14.00 |  |  |  |  |  |  |  |
| 14.00 – 15.00 |  |  |  |  |  |  |  |
| 15.00 – 16.00 |  |  |  |  |  |  |  |
| 16.00 – 17.00 |  |  |  |  |  |  |  |
| 17.00 – 18.00 |  |  |  |  |  |  |  |
| 18.00 – 19.00 |  |  |  |  |  |  |  |
| 19.00 – 20.00 |  |  |  |  |  |  |  |
| 20.00 – 21.00 |  |  |  |  |  |  |  |
| 21.00 – 22.00 |  |  |  |  |  |  |  |
| 22.00 – 23.00 |  |  |  |  |  |  |  |
| 23.00 – 24.00 |  |  |  |  |  |  |  |

When you have completed the chart, add up the symbols and fill in the graph on the next page. Reflect on the final graph and consider whether you feel it represents a balanced lifestyle.

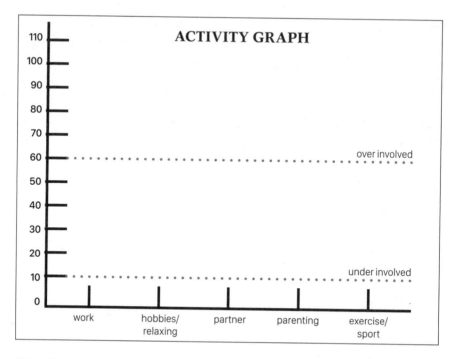

We all need different amounts of sleep but the minimum for most people is six uninterrupted hours per night. Children require between eight and ten, with teenagers requiring the most. If we are regularly getting less than six hours' uninterrupted sleep we need to address this by doing a sleep rota with our partner, taking naps during the day when our child sleeps or getting additional support. Similarly, if we are regularly sleeping for longer than ten hours we need to address this by making lifestyle changes. Adequate sleep is not only important for us to feel good about ourselves but it also impacts on our energy and mood. Sleep disruption, which is not caused by being woken, is important to address as early as possible in the parenting journey.

## Communication

One of the best and most effective ways of feeling good about ourselves is by communicating and being listened to. Talking and expressing ourselves physically and verbally and being listened to and heard by another person makes us feel valued. The ability to communicate requires learning and practice. Speaking and acting are the easiest parts, getting across what we really want to say or how we really feel is more complex.

To communicate effectively we need to be able to know what we want to express, how best to express it and how the person we are trying to communicate with understands us. Importantly, effective communication requires another person to listen, hear and understand what we are trying to express. Having some awareness of how good or bad we are at communicating, particularly regarding emotions, is the starting point. This gives us a foundation on which to build and grow. Acknowledging who we have in our lives to communicate with is also important and gives us the starting point from which we can enhance these relationships or build new ones.

The best communication involves a two-way process through which we express ourselves and the other person does the same. Central to feeling good about ourselves is the ability to communicate positive and negative things. While being able to communicate problems is vital, so too is being able to communicate the good things. Balance is essential. Communicating the positives and negatives of parenting keeps us healthy as parents. Communicating with our child is also important but this is not the place to discuss the ups and downs of life or our stresses and worries. In time our relationship with our child can emerge into this type of two-way support system but only when they are adults. Building our communication skills requires us to be honest and reflective with ourselves, ensuring we build these skills over time.

**EXERCISE: COMMUNICATION**

Take no more than three minutes to complete each of these questions as honestly as you can. Move on to the next question after three minutes and leave any you can't complete unanswered.

| 161 | Who do you talk to most in your life? |
|---|---|
| 162 | Who do you spend time with when you are happy? |
| 163 | Who do you spend time with when you are sad? |
| 164 | What topic do you find most difficult to discuss? |
| 165 | What would you like to be able to talk about that you don't feel you can? |
| 166 | Who likes to talk to you? |
| 167 | Who likes to spend time with you when they are happy? |
| 168 | Who likes to spend time with you when they are sad? |
| 169 | What do you find easy to listen to? |
| 170 | What do you find difficult to listen to? |

This exercise focuses on our communication opportunities and abilities. It asks us to consider who we communicate with and what changes we would like to make that we think could improve our communication skills. Our answers to these questions give us some indication of our strengths in this area and also help to reinforce the communication systems we have established.

Reflecting on difficult to answer or unanswered questions highlights for us areas that may require further development. Communication skills and networks evolve throughout our lifetime, so reflecting on these skills at any given moment in time helps us to continue to enhance them for ourselves. Having strong communication skills and healthy communication networks helps us to support our child to develop these skills and networks themselves.

## Building our own self-esteem

Having a positive set of beliefs about ourselves is an important component of being able to feel good about ourselves. Alongside loving ourselves and knowing we are loved and are lovable, we need to have a set of positive beliefs about ourselves. This serves to strengthen our emotional health and helps us deal better with emotional challenges. Our belief systems about ourselves are influenced by many things – our successes and failures, the feedback we receive and how we interpret all of these.

Building positive self-esteem is essential to our emotional well-being and involves hard work and insight. All of us have experiences that serve to make us feel negative about ourselves, and equally we all have experiences that make us feel positive. However, most everyday experiences can be interpreted positively if we have the willingness and ability to do this. Of course this is easier if as a child we have learnt to develop and nurture our self-esteem. It is, however, never too late, and becoming a parent provides us with a good opportunity to start or build on this process.

| EXERCISE: BUILDING OUR OWN SELF-ESTEEM | |
|---|---|
| Take no more than three minutes to complete each of these questions as honestly as you can. Move on to the next question after three minutes and leave any you can't complete unanswered. | |
| 171 | What is the most important decision you have made this week? |
| 172 | What is the most important parenting decision you have made this week? |
| 173 | What is the one thing that surprised you about yourself this week? |
| 174 | What thing did you get praised for this week? |
| 175 | What were you told you are good at most often this week? |
| 176 | What thing about your parenting did you get praised for this week? |
| 177 | What were you told you are good at as a parent most often this week? |
| 178 | What did your child say to you that made you feel good about yourself this week? |
| 179 | What did your child do this week that made you feel good about yourself? |
| 180 | What did your parent think you were good at when you were a child? |

This exercise asks us to reflect on our own self-esteem both as a parent and as an individual. Two questions in the exercise focus on how our child contributes to this self-esteem. Our answers help us to acknowledge our positive image of ourselves and some of our strengths and abilities. It also helps us acknowledge how our child can contribute to this self-esteem when we focus on the positive reinforcement he or she gives us.

Difficult to answer or unanswered questions suggest we may need to focus a little on this aspect of ourselves. They can also suggest that we find it difficult to see the positives in ourselves and that our opportunities for building our self-esteem are few. From this perspective, unanswered questions provide us with an opportunity to start to rebuild this aspect of ourselves and to start to give ourselves the opportunity to enhance our self-esteem.

Helping our child build strong self-esteem requires us to be sensitive to this aspect of ourselves and to have the skills and abilities to strengthen this if required.

## Being disciplined

Self-discipline plays an important part in our capacity to feel good about ourselves. Knowing that we can trust ourselves makes us feel more secure and confident. Self-discipline involves us trying our best to live to the rules and standards that we have set for ourselves. This usually involves decisions about our lifestyle, our use of alcohol, how we deal with anger and the moral and ethical decisions we make. When we become parents self-discipline becomes even more important because we know that we are a role model for our child and what we do has a direct influence on them. No matter how self-disciplined we are we never live up to our own standards all of the time. It is committing to trying to do this that makes us feel good about ourselves and particularly about ourselves as parents. Self-discipline is not about depriving or punishing ourselves; it is about trying to live to the standards we know will make us feel that we are good people.

| **EXERCISE: POSITIVE SELF-DISCIPLINE** | |
|---|---|
| Take no more than three minutes to complete each of these questions as honestly as you can. Move on to the next question after three minutes and leave any you can't complete unanswered. | |
| 181 | What action did you take this week that made you feel you had done the right thing? |
| 182 | What action did you take this week that you would prefer you hadn't? |
| 183 | What action did you take this week that indicates to yourself that you are disciplined? |
| 184 | What belief do you hold that helps you to be self-disciplined? |
| 185 | What action did you take this week that you would like your child to repeat? |
| 186 | What good example did you show to your child this week? |
| 187 | What one thing would you like to improve about your self-discipline? |

This exercise is designed to help us reflect on our positive discipline skills. Two of the questions deal directly with how we model discipline for our child. The answers to these questions reinforces for us the importance of self-discipline and how this makes us feel good about ourselves. Our answers also reinforce for us how important positive discipline is in supporting our child to develop good self-discipline.

Questions we found difficult or could not answer might suggest that this is an area we have not focused on sufficiently or that we find it hard to be self-disciplined. These can provide us with an opportunity to refocus on this area of our lives or to commence on our journey of improving our self-discipline.

Enhancing our child's positive self-discipline contributes significantly to their emotional welfare. Developing and practising these skills helps us to support our child in this key area of growth.

## Teaching spiritual and/or philosophical beliefs

We all need to believe that there is a greater purpose to our lives than just our everyday existence. This helps to motivate us and to make sense of adversity and sadness when we experience them. To be emotionally healthy we need to have healthy and positive spiritual and/or philosophical beliefs. This, like many other aspects of our development, is a lifelong journey. Giving ourselves the space and time to explore, develop and live our beliefs is important. This is particularly relevant to our parenting where making sense of our experiences and meeting challenges requires a belief in a greater purpose.

| EXERCISE: SPIRITUAL AND PHILOSOPHICAL BELIEFS | |
|---|---|
| Take no more than three minutes to complete each of these questions as honestly as you can. Move on to the next question after three minutes and leave any you can't complete unanswered. | |
| 188 | What one spiritual/philosophical thought did you have this week? |
| 189 | What one spiritual/philosophical belief do you hold that makes you feel happy? |
| 190. | What one spiritual/philosophical belief do you hold that makes you feel confident? |
| 191 | What one spiritual/philosophical belief do you hold that makes you feel confident about your parenting? |
| 192 | What one spiritual/philosophical belief do you hold that makes you want to do better? |
| 193. | What is the one most important spiritual/philosophical belief you have learnt or has been reinforced for you this week? |

This exercise helps us to consider our spiritual and philosophical beliefs. The area of spirituality is a complex one that requires significant discussion, so the purpose of this exercise is simply to remind us of the importance of spiritual and/ or philosophical beliefs both for ourselves and for our child.

The answers to the questions can provide us with the incentive to give more consideration, time and energy to these aspects of our lives. The answers can also reinforce the importance of helping our child to focus on these aspects of themselves.

Questions we did not answer or found difficult to answer serve as a reminder for us to refocus on this particular component of self-development. Feeling good about ourselves does not mean believing we are perfect or are better than others. It is the ability to recognise and appreciate our own strengths and weaknesses and our own distinct set of personality traits, skills and abilities. Feeling good about ourselves is essential to our emotional health and well-being.

## Ensuring the environment in which we live and parent is an emotionally healthy one

Creating a safe environment for ourselves in which we feel physically safe, respected and valued is essential to our emotional health and psychological well-being. This is particularly important for our parenting, which will thrive in an emotionally safe environment. We need to feel safe, secure and valued in our home, in work and when we socialise. Feeling unsafe, insecure or disrespected in any facet of our life will negatively impact on our emotional health and on our child's emotional health. In chapter five we discussed some of the skills involved in creating healthy environments.

We cannot control all of our experiences all of the time, and trying to will adversely affect our emotional health. We can, however, do all that is practical and reasonable to reduce the number of unnecessary adverse or negative experiences in our lives. Utilising the risk assessment process outlined in chapter five is useful to identify and monitor the risks that we come across in everyday life that could impact on our own emotional health. It helps to identify the risks that need to be addressed and the ones that we can live with. It is also useful to do this exercise at different times in our lives, particularly if we begin to get worried about a new development or if we are confronted with a worrying decision.

**Emotional health risk assessment**

The emotional risk assessment involves the following steps:

1. Write down all the issues that you are worried about regarding your own emotional health. Be as honest as you can. For instance: 'Work is becoming more difficult because my boss is giving me a very hard time and I am worried I will start to lose motivation and get stressed.'

2. Write down the main emotional or psychological effects that could or are happening as a result of this risk (the implications). For instance: 'I am beginning to feel stressed, worthless and depressed and I feel this could get worse.'

3. Rate how important this issue is to you on a scale of one to five, one being not at all important and five being very important. For instance: 'I need to work and usually enjoy it. So this is very important, five.'

4. Rate how likely this issue is to arise on a scale of one to five, one being not likely and five being very likely. 'Each week it seems to be getting worse and I am feeling stressed. Sometimes I don't feel like getting out of bed to go to work and I get into terrible form at weekends, thinking about work. Five.'

5. Calculate a risk score by multiplying the two scores together. An issue receiving a score of over twenty is one you need to take actions to address; one that receives between fifteen and twenty is worth monitoring; while anything rated lower can be dismissed. 'This risk is rated as a five by five equalling twenty five, therefore it needs to be addressed.'

6. Write down what you can do to address the risks you have identified as serious and keep this for the future. For instance: 'I am going to speak to HR and ask for a transfer to another section where I know the boss is easier to get on with.'

The following charts provide a useful means for conducting this assessment, although a blank piece of paper works equally well. The important thing is to have faith in your own judgement and to be brave enough to confront serious risks. We are all subject to dangers and risks. We cannot cripple ourselves by exaggerating these risks, but equally it is important that we identify the ones that are most serious and try to address them as best we can. Some risks we can do nothing about and part of this exercise is to identify these and then forget about them.

| Ref | Risk | Implications | Significance (A) | Likelihood (B) | Risk Score (C) | Actions to take |
|---|---|---|---|---|---|---|
| Example | Work is becoming more difficult because my boss is giving me a very hard time and I am worried I will start to lose motivation and get stressed. | I am beginning to feel stressed, worthless and depressed and I feel this could get worse. | 5 | 5 | 25 | I am going to speak to HR and ask for a transfer to another department where I know the boss is easier to get on with. |
| 1 | | | | | | |
| 2 | | | | | | |
| 3 | | | | | | |
| 4 | | | | | | |
| 5 | | | | | | |

It is important to review your top risks at a later date to see if the actions you have taken have changed things. If not you can come up with some new actions.

| TOP RISKS | | | | |
|---|---|---|---|---|
| Ref | Risk | Risk score three months ago | Risk score now | Change & purposed actions |
| Example | Losing interest and getting stressed in work. | 25 | (5 sig x 2 likl)=10 | Forget. |
| 1 | | | | |
| 2 | | | | |
| 3 | | | | |
| 4 | | | | |
| 5 | | | | |
| 6 | | | | |
| 7 | | | | |
| 8 | | | | |

## What if I am experiencing emotional difficulties?

No matter how well we nurture our emotional health and psychological well-being, approximately one in five of us will experience an emotional difficulty during our lifetime. Some of us will experience serious difficulties that can persist.

Accepting that we have difficulties and finding ways to deal with or recover from them is important. There are many obstacles preventing us from facing up to our difficulties, including stigma, worry that we may never be able to overcome them, and fear that we are letting our family or our child down.

Seeking to address our difficulties and accessing the required supports helps us to live more fruitful, enjoyable lives. This is most important for parents with emotional difficulties. While such parents can be just as good at parenting as those who don't have difficulties, having an emotional difficulty makes parenting more challenging and less enjoyable. It can also, if not addressed and managed, make it harder for our child to stay emotionally healthy. Dealing with our own emotional difficulties involves doing the following:

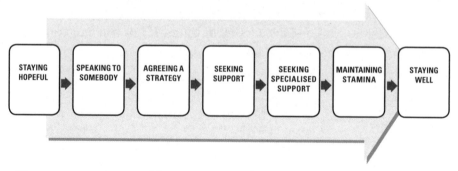

S1. STAYING HOPEFUL: If we are experiencing emotional difficulties, no matter how severe, we need to try to stay hopeful. While feelings of anxiety, panic, uncertainty and hopelessness might be part of the difficulties we need to try to remember that we can and will overcome them.

S2. SPEAKING TO SOMEBODY: It is imperative that we discuss our concerns with somebody we trust as soon as possible. We need to explore with them how we feel and why we think we feel this way. If we are acting in ways that are bothering or upsetting us we need to discuss this as well. Discussing our concerns will not only help us feel a little better but will also help clarify for ourselves how severe our difficulties might be. No matter how embarrassed, afraid or upset we are, keeping the conversation as practical, straightforward and honest as possible is important.

S3. AGREEING A STRATEGY: We need to agree a plan or a strategy to address our difficulties. We won't know exactly what might help, – if we did we would be taking these actions already – so we need to listen to what advice we are getting. If more advice is necessary we should try to seek this from a person we trust. Having taken the vital steps of acknowledging our difficulty and confiding in someone, it is very important that we agree a plan that we are committed to and can follow through on.

S4. SEEKING SUPPORT: If we believe we are experiencing emotional difficulties it is imperative that we seek support. What support we need and want will become clearer when we have confided in someone else and agreed a plan. The support of a friend or loved one might be enough, or we might need more formalised support. Again this step requires us to be brave enough to seek out and engage with the support option that we feel will help us effectively deal with our difficulty. The most effective support at this stage should focus on accepting and understanding our distress as real, reinforcing and helping us to draw off our emotional health and psychological resilience skills, reinforcing basic emotional management skills, and helping us address factors in our environment that are causing us distress.

S5. SEEKING SPECIALISED HELP: Sometimes no matter how much support we access our emotional difficulties are so severe that we need to seek out specialised help. If this occurs we first need to remember to stay hopeful. Many people require specialised care and again we know that this can be very effective in enabling us to overcome our challenges and live enjoyable lives. Accessing the right care is important. This specialised support and treatment can involve talking therapy, making changes to our environment, medication or a combination of all three. The combination of these interventions that work best is very much dependent on our particular difficulty and the evidence that supports different approaches for different difficulties. Once we think we need specialised help the first place we should go is to our family doctor. He/she is best placed to provide an initial assessment of our needs and to recommend the next steps.

S6. MAINTAINING STAMINA: Maintaining our energy and engagement in our recovery is vital to its success. Because difficulties affect both our behaviour and feelings, resolution of them is rarely straightforward. Remembering that overcoming our difficulties is not only possible but is to be expected is the key to maintaining our positivity and hope.

S7. STAYING WELL: When we begin feeling well after an episode of emotional difficulty we should feel happy and proud of ourselves. This is a time to celebrate our achievement and to take the opportunity to live and enjoy life. It is also a good time to put an 'Individual Emotional Health Enhancement Plan (IEHEP)' in place. This plan has four components:

- Developing an emotional health tool box;
- Outlining a daily emotional health plan for ourselves;
- Identifying triggers and early warning signs and a plan to deal with these;
- Agreeing an action plan for relapses.

Following a period of emotional difficulty it is natural for us to feel insecure; this sometimes makes us unsure of ourselves as parents. However, this is the time when it is most important to put into practice all of the skills of staying emotionally healthy, reminding ourselves again and again that we are good parents, that our child needs and loves us and if we can connect with our inner love for them we can overcome any challenge.

**Summary**

Keeping ourselves emotionally and psychologically healthy is essential to our own welfare and to our ability to enjoy and thrive as a parent. Achieving the balance with all of the demands of modern-day parenting takes awareness and commitment. Balancing our emotional welfare with our child's demands, needs and emotional welfare can also, at times, be a challenge. Achieving it not only enriches us but also enhances our relationships, particularly with our child. It is worth the effort.

# Conclusion

'Our parenting investment never ends because that's the way we want it to be and that's the commitment *our* children will give *their* children.'

Raising our child to be emotionally healthy is one of the most important tasks we will ever undertake. It defines the core purpose of parenting.

The rewards for our child are immense, giving him or her the best opportunity to live a happy, fulfilled life. With emotional health our child stands the best chance of making the most of their childhood and of growing to be a productive and happy adult. They will be the parent who is most likely to try to raise emotionally healthy children of their own.

For us, the rewards are also immense in seeing our child thriving and knowing that we have done our best for them. Connecting with our inner parent and investing in our child completes us as people. It reinforces our abilities, self-awareness and self-regard and enhances our emotional well-being.

The parenting journey is lifelong for our child and for us. It never ends and it is never too late. Along the way it is possible that we or our child will experience emotional difficulties. This is a challenge that can and should be overcome. Our understanding of such difficulties and how to recover from them is thorough and advanced. Applying what we know and taking the appropriate steps ensures that these difficulties are seen for what they are – 'bumps in the road'.

Throughout this book there are a number of exercises designed to help us gain insight into our child and ourselves. The answers we give to these are not definitive and will inevitably change as we progress through the parenting journey. From this perspective it is valuable to repeat the exercises from time to time.

While each exercise stands alone, some parents have found it useful to consider their answers in a more holistic way. Two approaches to doing this are presented at the end of this chapter.

I'm sure that for many parents this book will simply reinforce what they already know and are already doing. For others, I hope it will give them some help and encouragement to begin or reinvest in the most important journey they will ever embark upon. The message to take away is one of confidence, optimism and hope.

The book aims to establish how important you are to your child, the most important person in the world. I hope that after reading it you will appreciate the very special contribution you are making to your child's life by being prepared to give your all for them; the future richness and health of the society in which you live rests in your hands.

# My Personal Parenting Journey Exercises

**My Personal Parenting Development Graph**

This exercise is designed to help you consider your overall answers to the exercises contained throughout the book. It provides a mechanism to gauge the areas you have identified as being well developed and those you feel might benefit from more work. The exercise requires revisiting the exercises and recording the numbers of questions you answered to your satisfaction in each. The second part of the exercise requires you to add the numbers of questions you answered to your satisfaction under each of the headings as outlined below and entering your score on the parenting development graph. The trend of your own personal graph gives you a picture of what areas you believe are well developed and what areas you might want to develop further. Any scores falling below the graph line probably require further consideration and development. Scores significantly above the line may indicate particular areas of insight or strength. This exercise provides a snapshot of a given time and is therefore useful to repeat throughout the parenting journey.

**Finding Your Inner Parent score:** Add all the answers you were satisfied with to questions 1–25

**Teaching How To Be Happy score:** Add all the answers you were satisfied with to questions 26–48

**Teaching Self-Belief score:** Add all the answers you were satisfied with to questions 49–90

**Creating An Emotionally Healthy Environment score:** Add all the answers you were satisfied with to questions 91–127

**Looking After Ourselves score:** Add all the answers you were satisfied with to questions 12, 25, 42, 43, 51, 52, 56, 62, 64, 70, 79, 82, 83, 96, 128–193

**Having Insight Into Our Own Childhood score:** Add all the answers you were satisfied with to questions 13, 14, 15, 16, 57, 66, 71–75, 84, 87, 88, 90, 115, 125, 126, 127, 145, 180

**Parenting Confidence score:** Add all the answers you were satisfied with to questions 6, 9, 11, 17-25, 70, 82, 83, 116–193

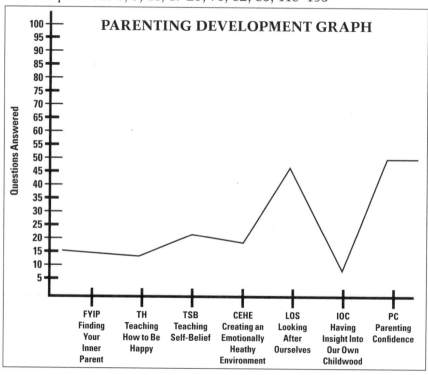

### My childhood story exercise

In researching this book I asked a number of people from different backgrounds to tell me the stories of their childhood. They found the process of remembering and sharing both insightful and refreshing. Recalling our own childhoods and how it might influence our parenting is useful for all of us to do when we are ready. This exercise provides one way of doing this. It involves writing freely under the headings on the next page and reflecting on your story when it is completed. Referencing your answers to the exercise questions throughout the book can be useful.

**Description of your childhood:** when you were born, how many siblings you had, any relevant life events, a parent dying, etc. what your parents worked at, where you went to school, what type of school you went to.

Events that made you feel loved by a parent:

Things your parents did that taught you how to be happy:

Things your parents did that taught you how to feel good about yourself:

If you had any difficulties in school or at home, what they were, how you overcame them or how they were resolved:

Why you think you are an emotionally healthy person now:

How you think your childhood experiences have impacted on your parenting:

• To read some of the childhood stories or to share your own story and any of your insights from the book go to www.workbook.ie.

# References

Bandura, A., *Social Learning Theory* (Englewood Cliffs, NJ: Prentice Hall, 1977).

Bowlby J., *Loss: Sadness & Depression. Attachment and Loss* (vol. 3) (International psycho-analytical library no. 109, London: Hogarth Press, 1980)

Brazelton, T. Berry and Cramer, Bertrand. G., *The Earliest Relationship: Parents, Infants and the Drama of Early Attachment* (H. Karnal Books Ltd).

Burns, R., *Self-concept Development and Education* (London: Holt, Rinehart and Winston, 1982).

Department of Health and Children, *State of the Nation's Children, Ireland* (Dublin: Government Publications, 2006).

Hibell, et al., 'Report-Alcohol and Other Drug Use amongst Students in 35 European Countries', *The ESPAD* (Sweden: The Swedish Council for Information on Alcohol and Other Drugs, 2003).

Hunt J., *The Natural Child: Parenting from the Heart* (Gabriola Island, British Columbia Canada: New Society Publishers, 2001).

Leach, P., *Your Baby and Child* (Penguin, 1988).

Jackson, L. A., von Eye, A., Biocca, F. A., Barbatsis, G., Zhao, Y., and Fitzgerald, H. E., *Children's Home Internet Use: Predictors and Psychological, Social and Academic Consequences*. The social impact of domestic computing and telecommunications. (London: Oxford University Press, 2004).

Kraut R., Patterson M., Lundmark V., Kiesler S., Mukopadhyay T., and Scherlis W., *Internet Paradox: A Social Technology that Reduces Social Involvement and Psychological Well-being?* (American Psychologist, 1998) September 53(9): 1017–31.

Seligman, M. E. P., *Helplessness: On Depression, Development, and Death* (San Francisco: W. H. Freeman, 1975).

Webwise survey of Children's Use of the Internet, Investigating Online Risk Behaviour (www.webwise.ie, 2006).

**Websites**

mayoclinic.org/healthy-living/childrens-health/in-depth/mental-illness-in-children/art-20046577

reachout.com/inform-yourself/